Most Illustrious Hereditary Prince...

LETTERS TO THEIR PRINCE FROM MEMBERS OF
THE HESSE-HANAU MILITARY CONTINGENT IN
THE SERVICE OF ENGLAND DURING THE
AMERICAN REVOLUTIONARY WAR

TRANSLATED BY
Bruce E. Burgoyne

PREPARED WITH THE VALUED ASSISTANCE OF
Marie E. Burgoyne

FROM TOM VIII OF THE LIDGERWOOD COLLECTION
IN ARCHIVES OF THE MORRISTOWN NATIONAL HISTORICAL PARK

HERITAGE BOOKS
2013

HERITAGE BOOKS
AN IMPRINT OF HERITAGE BOOKS, INC.

Books, CDs, and more—Worldwide

For our listing of thousands of titles see our website
at
www.HeritageBooks.com

Published 2013 by
HERITAGE BOOKS, INC.
Publishing Division
100 Railroad Ave. #104
Westminster, Maryland 21157

Copyright © 2003 Bruce E. Burgoyne

All rights reserved. No part of this book may be reproduced or transmitted in any form or by any means, electronic or mechanical, including photocopying, recording or by any information storage and retrieval system without written permission from the author, except for the inclusion of brief quotations in a review.

International Standard Book Numbers
Paperbound: 978-0-7884-2375-8
Clothbound: 978-0-7884-6921-3

HERITAGE BOOKS, INC.

Other books by the author:

Waldeck Soldiers of the American Revolutionary War
Diaries of Two Ansbach Jaegers
The Hesse-Cassel Mirbach Regiment in the American Revolution
The 3rd English-Waldeck Regiment in the American Revolution
Georg Pausch's Journal and Reports of the Campaign in America
Enemy Views: The American Revolutionary War
as Recorded by the Hessian Participants
Eighteenth Century America: A Hessian Report On the People, the Land,
the War As Noted in the Diary of Chaplain Philipp Waldeck (1776-1780)
The Diary of Lieutenant von Bardeleben
and other von Donop Regiment Documents
Defeat, Disaster, and Dedication
Canada During the American Revolutionary War
A Hessian Officer's Diary of the American Revolution

Letters to the Prince

INTRODUCTION

Most Illustrious Hereditary Prince is my translation of "Letters and Reports from Hesse-Hanau Officers, 1776-80", a document in the Lidgerwood Collection of the Morristown National Historical Park Archives, made under a grant from the Eastern National Park and Monument Association. Actually, the letters, primarily from officers of the Hesse-Hanau Hereditary Prince Regiment, covers letters written as late as the return march to Hanau, in 1783. It is hoped that it will enable Americans who do not read German to get a better understanding of the American Revolutionary War and of the men who fought against the colonists.

Six minor German states sold troops (the Hessians) into English service for use against the American colonists. Those states were Anhalt-Zerbst, Ansbach-Bayreuth, Brunswick, Hesse-Cassel, Waldeck, and Hesse-Hanau.

The prince in the title of this translation was the Count of Hanau. As the son of the Landgrave of Hesse-Cassel and an English princess, he was also the Hereditary Prince of Hesse-Cassel, and upon the death of his father, he became Wilhelm IX, Landgrave of Hesse-Cassel.

His original domain of Hesse-Hanau, on the Rhine River, was not large, but still provided a total of 2,257 men to the English effort. In 1776 an infantry

Letters to the Prince

regiment and an artillery company, 796 men, were sent to Canada. The next year, a jaeger battalion was sent to Canada, and in 1782, a free corps infantry regiment was sent to New York. Each year recruit shipments were sent from Europe to replace men who had been killed, died, deserted, or who were recalled to Germany.

Each company was allowed to take six women, women who served as nurses, cooks, washerwomen, and even beasts of burden. These women provided the support elements required by the modern army. They were not the so-called camp-followers of lowly reputation, but most were the wives of company soldiers. If a woman's husband died, they had to marry another soldier or be sent back to Germany.

When General John Burgoyne began his march south toward Albany from Canada in 1777, he took most of the German soldiers from Canada, but left a force of 600 men behind, a force composed of men from various German units, many of whom were sick or unable to participate in a strenuous campaign. In the Battle of Bennington, two companies of Brunswick troops suffered serious losses, as did the Hanau artillery detachment which accompanied them. The following pages contain letters from three artillery officers, Spangenberg, Bach, and Dufais. These men, prisoners after the Battle of Bennington, were not considered the same as men taken after Burgoyne's capitulation, men known as Convention prisoners. However, many ordinary prisoners of war were held with the Convention prisoners, first near Boston, and then, after a long march, they were held in barracks near Charlottesville, Virginia.

The period covered by the letters is not 1776 to 1780, but actually to 1783. The letters cover many of the events and activities in which the Leib, or Body, Company, of the Hereditary Prince Regiment participated. Two of the letters, in French, were not translated, but may be found in the German manuscript in the Morristown archives in Morristown, New Jersey.

In making this translation, I have taken the liberty of breaking some of the long, involved German sentences and paragraphs into shorter, more easily understood segments. I have also reduced the length and frequency of the ornate expressions used in referring to the ruler of Hesse-Hanau. Finally, I have used a number of sources in an effort to more closely identify individuals, with most of the identifying material being taken from the "Rainsford Papers" of the British Museum Additional Manuscripts, volumes 23649 to 23651.

Bruce E. Burgoyne
Dover, DE
January 2003

Letters to the Prince

Table of Contents

Introduction   i

Letters from Captain Friedrich von Germann to the Hereditary Prince   1
    Enclosure - Letter from Lieutenant Colonel Michael von Janecke to Lieutenant Colonel Johann Christoph Lentz and his reply   26

Letters from Captains von Germann and Friedrich Ludwig von Schoell, and Lieutenant Maurice von Buttlar to the Hereditary Prince   29

Note about a letter in French, not included, from Captain von Germann to The Hereditary Prince   30

Letters from Lieutenant Friedrich von Geismar to the Hereditary Prince   31
    Enclosure - Order to Captain von Geismar from Colonel Wilhelm Rudolph von Gall   36

Letters from Major Ludwig Wilhelm von Passern to the Hereditary Prince   36

Letters to the Prince

Letters from Captain von Schoell to the Hereditary Prince	38
Enclosure - Description of a Maneuver	62
Letters from Staff Captain Christian von Eschwege to the Hereditary Prince	77
Enclosure - March Route Bremerlehe to Witzhause	110
Letters from Lieutenant Carl von Lindau to the Hereditary Prince	114
Letters from Lieutenant von Buttlar to the Hereditary Prince	123
Letters from Captain Friedrich von Schachten to the Hereditary Prince	140
Letters from Lieutenant Wilhelm Dufais to the Hereditary Prince	142
Letter from Free Corporal Franz von Pape to the Hereditary Prince	149
Letter from Lieutenant Zincke to the Hereditary Prince	150

Letters to the Prince

Letter from Adjutant Jacob Heerwagen to the Hereditary Prince — 152

Letter from Lieutenant Friedrich Ludwig Kempffer to the Hereditary Prince — 154

Letter from the Hesse-Hanau Officers to the Hereditary Prince — 155

Letter from Carl Ludwig Theodor Burckhard to the Hereditary Prince — 156

Letter from Captain-at-arms Adam Kirchoff to the Hereditary Prince — 160

Letter from Quartermaster Sergeant Andreas Koch to the Hereditary Prince — 163

Letters from Lieutenant Carl Dittmar Spangenberg to the Hereditary Prince — 163
   Enclosure - Attestation by Regimental Surgeon Jeremiah Heidelbach — 166

Letters to the Prince

Letter from Lieutenant Spangenberg
to the Court Marshal — 167

Letter from Lieutenant Johann
Michael Bach to the Court Marshal — 172

Letter from Lieutenant Bach to
the Hereditary Prince — 177
    Enclosure - Attestation by
    Major Georg Pausch — 182

Note about a letter written in
French (not included) by
le Blanc — 182

Letter from Captain Jost Friedrich
von Francke to the Hereditary
Prince — 183

Letters from Lieutenant von Buenau
to the Hereditary Prince — 184

Letter from Regimental Quartermaster Carl August Sartorius to
the Hereditary Prince — 187

Letter from Bombardier Johann
Moerschell to the Hereditary Prince — 189

Letters to the Prince

Most Illustrious Hereditary Prince, Gracious Sovereign and Lord!

May it please Your Highness to see in the attached report that there are only two individuals in the company who are sick, and who I hope will soon return to duty, as [Georg] Kohlep has almost recovered. In addition to the report, Musketeers [Henrich] Fischer and [Henrich] Eidebenz were also sick, but are now fully recovered. Quartermaster Sergeant [Henrich] Lenz has claimed for a few days of having a fever and chills, but I think it may only be diarrhea and not serious. At the muster held yesterday at Nijmegen the company was complete. This morning we exchanged ships for ones from Holland and each company was assigned two. The situation on board these is much better than on those, but warm food, tea, or coffee is just not to be had. On the first ship, I arranged at once so that the men could have warm meals, and did everything in my power to ensure tea and such for the sick. The troops are all happy and cheerful, and spend most of their time singing. To the present I have not seen a sour face in the company. I have every reason to be fully satisfied with Lieutenants [Maurice] von Buttlar and [Christian] von Eschwege, and hope that Ensign [Ernst] von Weyhers will follow their example. All the officers of the company lay themselves at Your Highness' feet and ask, as I do, most humbly for Your Highness'

Letters to the Prince

continued favor. I shall continue to strive to merit such, and to demonstrate that I remain with the most sincere affection.

In the region　　Your Serene Highness
of Bommel　　　My most gracious sovereign
23 March 1776　and Lord's most humble
　　　　　　　　and devoted servant.
　　　　　　　　F[riedrich] von Germann

- - - - - - -

Most Illustrious Hereditary Prince, Gracious Sovereign and Lord!

Your Highness, I submit herewith my most humble report, that I arrived here at Quebec with the company entrusted to me, on 1 June, at six o'clock in the evening. All the non-commissioned officers and privates are well, which is surprising considering our exceptionally long and very unpleasant voyage, and the poor rations. Your Highness, I will not give a brief summary of the misery we had to tolerate until now, as your will be able to understand that from the recorded events.

All the officers of the company lay themselves at Your Highness' feet, and humbly request your continued gracious favor, as does he, who with the most sincere respect strives to be

On the transport ship　Your Serene Highness
The Three Sisters　　 My Most Gracious
3 June 1776　　　　　　Sovereign and Lord's

Letters to the Prince

> Most humble servant,
> F. von Germann

- - - - - - - -

Most Illustrious Hereditary Prince, Gracious Sovereign and Lord!

Your Highness should not take it amiss, not to have received a report about the company so graciously entrusted to me. A long and dangerous illness and my absence from the company are the causes which kept me from my most humble duty. On the eighth of this month I rejoined the company at St. Culberth, from Montreal. According to the reported events, and as nearly as I could determine the truth during this short time, I hope that these winter quarters will restore the company from the sustained fatigue. Other than the two sick individuals, the rest of the troops are in good condition, and therefore I do not anticipate any loss due to sickness. Concerning the deaths, nothing more could be done. The regimental surgeon [Jeremiah Heidelbach] gave them his full attention, but nevertheless could not save them, and I, as with all the sick, as long as they were with the company, sought to relieve them; in part with money, in part with such refreshments as possible.

May Your Highness honor me with your continued graciousness and satisfaction, and be assured that I strive with most sincere devotion and eternal loyalty to be

Letters to the Prince

St. Culberth
10 November 1776

Your Serene Highness
Most Gracious Sovereign
and Lord's Most humble
servant,
F. von Germann

- - - - - - - -

Most Illustrious Hereditary Prince, Gracious
Sovereign and Lord!

Your Highness has, as was reported to my great shock by Colonel [Wilhelm Rudolph] von Gall, expressed displeasure with me because you received no humble report concerning the company entrusted to me, for such a long time. Your Highness will, as I may confidently hope, not hold it against me, if Your Highness will favorably consider accepting my well-founded excuse. Immediately upon my arrival in winter quarters, I did not fail humbly to report the condition of the company, after a prolonged illness, during which I spent three months at La Prairie in the camp at Savanne, and part at Montreal. I mentioned that it had made me completely incapable of performing the responsibilities of company commander, as Your Highness will have seen, in my last humble correspondence. During the past winter, no letter could be sent from here because of the ice, and I had no knowledge of the first packet boat sent from here in April. Your Highness, I can most humbly assure you that the company is in condition as good as when in Hanau. Not only did it drill well at La Prairie during the past summer, but also, during the recently held review, Major General [Friedrich Adolf] von Riedesel told me that the Leib Company, especially as to appearance, had a great advantage, not only over the other companies of its own regiment, but also over the Brunswick Corps. In addition to the changes in the report, the Hautboist [Andreas] Emmert received permission and made an advantageous marriage. Corporal Vaupel has so greatly changed, to his advantage, that I can report in all honesty, that he is one of the best non-commissioned officers in the company. As of now there are absolutely no sick individuals in the company, but the troops are all completely well and already have made a rather good start at drill. Lieutenants von Buttlar and Eschwege carry out their responsibility as industriously as before. Your Highness will (as I flatter myself with the confident hope) not find inadmissible this most humbly presented excuse, and will extend your favor, which I have most gratefully enjoyed prior to this time, graciously in the future.

With the most humble confidence I suggest to Your Highness with most sincere respect that in the entire army every commanding officer of the Leib Company would enjoy the benefits of a full captain. I have been entrusted with the command of your company for six years already, and you honored me

Letters to the Prince

with your satisfaction.

Furthermore, I will exert all my efforts, in so far as possible, to continue to earn this trust, and consider it a special good fortune if you would consider me worthy of being granted command of a company, should a company of the regiment become vacant. As I must now, in this position, unavoidably lay out more than a staff captain of any other company finds necessary, with no additional income to offset it. Your Highness will not note with disfavor when I venture to most humbly request Your Highness to consider, when looking back on the pressing circumstances, graciously granting me the benefit of a full captain.

Your Highness, I recommend myself most humbly, to the Father of my Country's constant favor and grace, and strive to be with the most vigorous application of sincere respect and thankfulness

    St. Culberth   Your Serene Highness
    13 May 1777   My Gracious Sovereign and
                            Lord's most humble servant
                            F. von Germann

Letters to the Prince[1]

Most Illustrious Hereditary Prince, Gracious Sovereign and Lord

Your Highness, I most humbly report herewith that after we received the order yesterday afternoon to break camp, the company moved out of its previous quarters this morning, the second of June, and rejoined the regiment at Berthier. We are to remain here until the fourth, when the march is to be resumed over Sorel and Chambly to Cumberland Head, the main assembly point for the army. Lieutenant von Buttlar is to take the heavy equipment to Three Rivers tomorrow. There is not a single soldier in the company who does not sincerely wish to meet the enemy, and all those detached to remain here in Canada show considerable disappointment about that. This attitude will earn the regiment more honors if we have the good fortune to engage the enemy this year.

The company is especially, as a result of the drill, in the best condition. Already for some time, I have not found it necessary to drill lazy or clumsy individuals. If Your Highness could, as I often but fruitlessly wish, actually observe this, we would all be pleased to have Your Highness' gracious satisfaction.

Your Highness, the parents and relatives of the regiment demonstrated their greatest pleasure when I introduced the company to them. Every heart swelled with the most sincere joy and appreciation, so that I do not doubt that each one will also gladly give his last

Letters to the Prince

drop of blood in the service of his gracious prince.

Sergeant Major [Samuel] Vaupel, with whom, as previously, I had every reason to be satisfied, thanks Your Highness most humbly for the gracious display of your favor toward himself and his wife. Musketeer [Conrad] Krieg received consent for his marriage with the widow left behind by Musketeer Schubert [possibly Johann Schauberger].

The company officers lay themselves at Your Highness' feet and wish, like me, to have the opportunity to earn Your Highness' favor.

With the most sincere respect, I strive to be

Berthier   Your Serene Highness
2 June 1777   My most gracious Sovereign and
                    Lord's most humble servant
                    F. von Germann

Most Illustrious Hereditary Prince, Gracious
      Sovereign and Lord

Your Highness, herewith I most humbly report that on 19 June I was sent from Cumberland Head to pick up the recruits for your regiment. I met them, under sail, at Sorel, but as they had orders to debark at Montreal, it was necessary for me to go there, also. I waited there impatiently for a few days and because the transport ships could sail no further than Varennes, because of contrary winds, I had to go back and allow the troops to land between Pointe aux Trembles and

Letters to the Prince

Varennes. This assignment, because of the terrible costs, was very expensive, and because of much discontent and inexperience of the non-commissioned officers, was very difficult. [Georg] Spengler was the first one that I had to punish, because of his bad mouth; the same resulted for Artillery Sergeant [Carl Friedrich] Hestermann, because of his gross negligence in service. These two examples worked so well that I finally accomplished my mission, and delivered all the recruits to the Saw Mill on 9 July. I had to take Lieutenant von Meyer of the Jaeger Corps to the regiment in arrest.

Quartermaster Sergeant [Carl Friedrich] Zipf did everything possible within his ability, and I can find no fault with Free Corporal [Franz] von Pape, either. Furthermore, I hope in time that he will develop very well. Other than the report, there is no illness in the company. [Hieronymus] Schweinsberger did not feel well for a few days, but has now recovered completely. I do not think that he will get sick very easily, as he eats with me every day. He is still the best and most professional soldier in the regiment. Lieutenant von Buttlar is temporarily in command of the Colonel's Company. I did not appreciate losing Quartermaster Sergeant Vaupel. He was very efficient at whatever was needed. It will be equally bad to lose Sergeant [Heinrich] Orth. Recruit [Michael] Remmy was transferred to the Leib Company.

Letters to the Prince

Yesterday evening the regiment reached a thick woods, where it camped. I have completely forgotten the name of the place, however.

Your Highness, please graciously forgive my poor handwriting because of the great haste, and furthermore, grant your continued favor to him who strives with the most sincere respect to be

11 July [1777]   Your Serene Highness
My most gracious Sovereign
and Lord's
Most humble servant
F. von Germann

- - - - - - -

Most Illustrious Hereditary Prince, Gracious Sovereign and Lord

Your Highness will not take amiss my last rather disorderly letter. The haste to report the condition of the company, and the short time I had therefore, were the cause. I wanted to report most humbly to Your Highness from Montreal onward, that I had left the regiment to pick up the recruits. But the often very unpleasant business would not allow me to do my most humble duty. Of those recruits assigned to the Leib Company, [Johann] Hermann and Spengler are the worst. I am quite satisfied with the others, especially [Adolph] Zehner. Although all the bad living conditions locally do not set well with them, the discontent has subsided as they understand that I used other means while on the march here, using all possible military persuasion and a frequent extra portion of brandy so that it is possible to more easily control the troops. Meanwhile, no one here, while I have been with the company, has received a single blow. [This probably means no one has been punished by running the gauntlet or being struck with the flat of a sword. It might also mean that there were no duels.] [Peter] Ewald was taken from the command due to illness. He is suffering from scurvy. If we had marched earlier, he would have died without hope of recovery. Now he is improving daily. As long as he was with the company, he took his meals with me. The regimental surgeon and [Wilhelm] Gottschalk also did everything possible for him, for which I give both of them credit, especially at the Leib Company.

The loss of Sergeant Orth makes me very unhappy. He and Quartermaster Sergeant Vaupel, after the sergeant major, were the best non-commissioned officers in the company. Now it is Quartermaster Sergeant Lentz. Sergeant [Philipp] Schaeffer is still in Canada. [Friedrich] Boeckel would be fairly good but he has too much ambition. Your Highness may be surprised that I would complain about that, especially when the situation with the soldiers is so critical, but I have good reason because the presumptuous thought which he has, to become an officer, causes him to do his captain-at-arms duty in an unpleasant manner.

Corporal [Jacob] Haumann is rather indolent, and Corporal [Peter] Weber, since his illness, has not fully recovered. I can not say much about Corporal Ewald; I hope that he will develop well If Free Corporal von Pape continues, as he has begun, I have good reason to be fully satisfied with him. Within the company, he is always very forthcoming and especially correct.

During their long voyage the recruits have completely forgotten their drill. I have been ordered to drill the entire transport daily, and I hope to have them in good condition in a short time. In addition to the report, men are reported sick daily, but they also recover quickly.

Your Highness, to give a humble report on the maintenance of the company, I must report that the uniforms are now in a poor condition. I have exchanged the best coats from the dead , and provided patches for the rest of the company. However, it will take much effort to maintain them until the coming spring. White linen is simply not to be bought in this country. I am glad that I was able to get what was necessary for the company from the regiment. Leather is likewise terribly expensive so that a pair of shoes costs over four gulden. I have had overalls made for the troops from the old tents. These are worn by the whole army, and in this land, because of the mosquitoes and other insects, they are very necessary. Among the new tents there was also a captain's tent provided for the Leib Company, but as you, Your Highness, are the captain of the company, and not a single staff captain received his own tent, and because of the extreme expense, I can not afford one on my pay, I accepted it on the condition that I await Your Highness' gracious order concerning payment therefore.

As no roster is available in the regiment, the accompanying rank list could only be made by guess. Therefore, Your Highness, do not take the incompleteness of this list unfavorably. Your Highness, I recommend myself most humbly to your continued favor, and strive with most sincere respect to be

    Skenesborough   Your Serene Highness
    26 July 1777   My most gracious sovereign
                          And Lord's
                          Most humble servant,
                          F. von Germann

- - - - - - -

Your Highness, herewith I must humbly report that today, 27 July, at four o'clock in the afternoon, Musketeer Jacob Schmidt has the misfortune to drown in the river flowing before the camp. He desired to wash his clothes, and to bathe at the same time. Unfortunately, he stepped into a depth into which he immediately sank. I at once sent men, and several Englanders, in a batteau, also went, to pull him out if

possible, but all their efforts were in vain.
F. von Germann

- - - - - - -

Most Illustrious Hereditary Prince, Gracious Sovereign and Lord!

Your Highness, it would give me the greatest joy if I could provide welcome news about the condition of the company, but in our present situation this is not possible. We live in a land where everything is lacking, and the officers as well as the soldiers, must do without the most necessary things. Everything that was surplus in this wild and underdeveloped land, the rebels have consumed, so that it is necessary for everyone to be content with the royal provisions - which consist of salted and often half-rotted meat and flour. Transportation is attended with endless difficulties, as all the food stuff and clothing can only be brought here from Canada. Therefore, in our situation, everything gravitates to the headquarters; we very seldom have the luck to receive anything, and then we must pay for it with cash. Your Highness, please allow me to give only a few items as an example of what the soldiers need, that is, tobacco and brandy. The first cost from four shillings a packet, and the latter equally as much for a bottle of cheap rum. Yes, it is necessary for most of the men to smoke dried leaves from the trees, and this is the case with everything. Meantime, we flatter ourselves with the

Letters to the Prince

vain hope that when we move further forward, our fate will change.

Your Highness will be so good as to notice in the accompanying report that there are only three sick individuals, except for those in the hospital, in the company. I am surprised by that, as the local climate and the necessary way of life must of necessity cause much illness, because we must tolerate a nearly unbearable heat during the day, and a great coldness at night, which with our severe shortages of equipment is very significant.

As the drowned Musketeer Schmidt's surviving widow, with her children, is unable to earn her livelihood without other support, I have continued to allow her the regular provisions, in the hope that Your Highness will not consider such unfavorably.

    With the most sincere respect, I strive to be

In camp near	Your Serene Highness
John's House	My most gracious Sovereign
29 August 1777	and Lord's
	Most humble servant,
	F. von Germann

- - - - - - -

Letters to the Prince

Most Illustrious Hereditary Prince
Gracious Sovereign and Lord

Your Highness will have seen in the last most humble report from John's House, our then unpleasant situation. This has since then daily worsened until we have reached the epitome of misery. From John's House we marched over Fort Edward, Fort Miller, the Batten Kill, and Saratoga to Freeman's, where General [Horatio] Gates awaited us at the head of an army four times stronger than ours, in a well-entrenched camp. Our position was so advantageous that the enemy dared not attack, and certainly we could now be in Albany, or even farther, especially if the recent unfortunate affair of 7 October had not taken place. During that affair, Musketeer [Ludwig] Hoene was shot through the body and lay dead on the spot. Corporal Ewald was twice wounded, once in the chest, and the other in the hip. Musketeer [Georg Carl] Ungar received a grazing shot to the neck, and [Johann] Sickenberger, a ball in the right foot. All three now have completely recovered. Your Highness, please allow me to briefly mention the conduct of Corporal Ewald. To the present he has always sought to out-perform all others in devotion to duty, and his behavior at other times is equally faultless. Musketeer [Georg] Tempell, who was sick and left behind during the retreat from Freeman's Farm, and until now I have received no information about him. Our tents and a large amount of gear was lost, so that during the following time, when we were between Batten Kill and Fish Kill, we had to lie out under the open sky. Here, the enemy surrounded us and harassed us daily with cannon and small arms fire, until finally General [John] Burgoyne surrendered the entire corps as prisoners of war on 17 October. The same day we were moved to Freeman's Farm, and the bad, often even more than vile, meeting of our enemy - whom during the whole march we had to endure - already began, by tearing from the bodies the cartridge straps and pouches belonging to the troops on duty with the equipment. Despite the raw weather and the often unbearable bad roads, the inhabitants were very seldom so sympathetic as to grant use of their barns for night quarters. On the other hand, they exerted every effort, by advantageous promises, to entice our troops into deserting. True, many soldiers remained behind during the march, but only because of exhaustion and a scarcity of small clothing. Still, after only a short time, they rejoined the company. [Johann] Rosenberger remained behind during the march from Nobletown to Barrington. [Michael] Herber deserted at the latter place on the morning of 26 October, after company roll call, shortly before marching away.

    Free Corporal von Pape, who had been sick for some time, remained behind on 5 November, during

Letters to the Prince

the march from Marlborough. Spengler, who deserted from the barracks on 11 November, reportedly, as I later heard, prevented the free corporal from returning by the bad description of our quarters. We arrived here at Winter Hill, a half-hour from Boston, on 7 November. The barracks in which we lie have been put together with planks and are exceptionally bad. The officers, in this respect, do not have the least advantage. Very narrow confines have been established for us, as to how far we can go, and everywhere we are watched by a large number of guards. However, they can not, or will not, bother us. Some of us have had their horses stolen, as I have had the misfortune to lose my best horse at this place.

Immediately after our arrival, I took care of my first problem, putting the small clothing, most of which were worn out, in good condition. Because of the unheard of cost this caused a very great expense. Despite tolerating the fatigue, the troops are all healthy, except for Koehler, and [Andreas] Kraft, who have nothing serious.

Your Highness, I most humbly recommend myself to your continued favor, and strive with the most sincere devotion to be Your Serene Highness

Winter Hill
7 December 1777

My most gracious Sovereign
And Lord's
Most humble servant,
F. von Germann

Letters to the Prince

Most Illustrious Hereditary Prince, Gracious Sovereign and Lord!

May it please Your Highness to see in the accompanying report that there has been no major change in your company since the last report, except for the recent desertion of Musketeer Hermann. Apparently his fellow countryman, the former song leader Angersbach, who has taken service with the Americans, has led him into this step.

Musketeer [Christopher] Wiskemann, whose discharge year had already passed on 10 December 1777, sought his most honorable discharge, declaring that if Your Highness would do this favor, of paying him a new bonus, he was ready to enter a new enlistment, and left it to Your Highness' pleasure how much you would allow. Sergeant Major Vaupel and Private [Georg Conrad] Fuhr have the fever, but I hope that nothing serious will result therefrom.

Your Highness, I recommend myself most humbly to your continued favor and strive with the most sincere devotion to be

    Winter Hill   Your Serene Highness
    9 May 1778   My most gracious Sovereign
                           And Lord's
                           Most humble servant,
                           F. von Germann

Letters to the Prince

Most Illustrious Hereditary Prince, Gracious Sovereign and Lord!

Your Highness, I must most humbly report that Lieutenant von Buttlar has been graciously promoted to staff captain and transferred to Colonel von Gall's Company, and Lieutenant von Trott, of the Grenadier Company, has been transferred here as a 1st lieutenant. However, the first had demonstrated such dedication to duty when assigned to this company, that I wish Lieutenant von Trott would follow his example. Sergeant Major Vaupel has suffered so much from his illness, that I feared for his life. He is now returned to duty, however, but is still very weak. Musketeer Remmy is also healthy again. That pleases me all the more as that individual, as long as he has been assigned to the company, has conducted himself exceptionally well. [Philipp] Bruckmann is recovering, and as I confidently hope, is out of all danger.

I must humbly thank Your Highness for the favor that was recently shown to my nephew. I hope he will merit it by his best possible conduct; at least, it will certainly not fail to support me. We were again led to believe that there will be an early exchange. May Heaven make it so, that we are soon released from our present misery, and returned to a useful position.

I most humbly recommend myself to Your Highness' favor, and remain in most sincere devotion

Letters to the Prince

Winter Hill
11 October 1778

Your Serene Highness
My most gracious Sovereign
And Lord's
Most humble servant,
F. von Germann

- - - - - - -

Most Illustrious Hereditary Prince, Gracious Sovereign and Lord!

May it please Your Highness, to see in the accompanying report and lists, the effective strength of the present body of troops. Except for the desertion of Musketeer [Conrad] Krebs, since my last most humble report, there has been no change in the company.

The company baggage left behind in Canada has finally arrived here. However, all my joy, occasioned thereby, was washed away when I found that nothing was the least bit serviceable from my own belongings, nor even from the company's small clothing. That loss, in our present situation, is even more unbearable as it is difficult to buy items of clothing here. Meanwhile, I have done everything in my power, to provide the most necessary items of small clothing for the men, and sought to at least keep them on a level with the other companies of the regiment.

I most humbly recommend myself to Your Highness' continued favor, and strive with the most sincere devotion to be

Letters to the Prince

Charlottesville   Your Serene Highness
19 September 1779   My most gracious Sovereign
                         And Lord's
                         Most humble servant,
                         F. von Germann

- - - - - - -

Most llustrious Hereditary Prince, Gracious Sovereign and Lord!

May it please Your Highness to see in the most humble reports accompanying, that on 19 September last year, that, except for Private [Wilhelm] Grimm, your company suffered no losses. That is all the more surprising to me as the men, up to now, because of a scarcity of provisions, have had to put up with so much. Now everyone hopes once again for an exchange in the near future, of which there are definite reports. If this hope is again groundless, I fear that the desertions will be even more numerous next summer than ever before. The company has been supplied with small clothing items as best possible, and all the troops are healthy, which is suprising in our present situation.

I recommend myself to Your Highness' continued favor, and strive, with the most sincere devotion, to be

At the barracks   Your Serene Highness
At Charlottesville   My most gracious Sovereign
29 Februauary 1780   And Lord's
                       Most humble servant,

Letters to the Prince

F. von Germann

- - - - - - -

Most Illustrious Hereditary Prince, Gracious Sovereign and Lord!

During the time that I have been in Your Highness' service, it has always been my effort, by diligence and loyalty, to make myself worthy of Your Highness' service. I acknowledge the sign of Your Highness' favor with the most humble thanks, that it has pleased Your Highness to award the Grenadier Company to me, and I will untiringly strive, through the most sincere devotion, to earn that great honor. Captain [Friedrich] von Schachten, who commanded the company previously, requests, therefore, until his return to Germany, to draw a captain's pay, and such would be denied me, from the time it was Your Highness' pleasure to award the company to me. However, I am so fully convinced of Your Highness' sense of justice that I doubted my enjoyment of the prerogatives and benefits, which the commission promises, for only a moment, and I am furthermore so assured of the gracious increase of salary, I let that of staff captain of the Leib Company drop at once, when it was Your Highness' gracious intention that I was to have the enjoyment of a full captain's pay from the time I was given the position of grenadier captain. The withdrawl of such would make me the only sufferer and loser, as the others who were advanced by my promotion, such as Lieutenant Eschwege and Ensign [Ludwig Theodor] Burckhard, received first lieutenant and ensignn appointments, while I have lost hereby the staff captain appointment in the Brunswick establishment, from 1 June 1776 until 1778, should I return what was received on 1 October 1778.

All the reasons for my requerst, I lay at the feet of the best and most gracious prince, and await from him the decision, if what the favor of my prince promised me should be taken away, and the fair and legitimate be denied me.

    With the most sincere devotion, I strive to be
Albemarle Couny   Your Serene Highness
10 May 1780   My most gracious Sovereign
    And Lord's
    Most humble servant,
    F. von Germann

Most Illustrious Hereditary Prince, Gracious Sovereign and Lord!

Lieutenant Colonel [Michael] von Janecke, of the Hesse-Hanau Free Corps, on the fifth of this month, sent a letter to Colonel [Johannn Christoph] Lentz, of the 1st Battalion, in which he reported that Captain [Carl August] Scheel, who was advanced to major and transferred to the mentioned free corps, was very drunk upon his arrival there, and openly declared to various officer of the Free Corps, that supposedly I had said about the mentioned Major Scheel, that officers of the 1st Battalion refused duty with him, and that he had supposedly been threatened with flogging if he did not request his release. However, both are groundless.

Major Scheel was, while we were still in captivity in Virginia, given to drunkenness, and the then commander of the 1st Battalion, Colonel von Gall, assigned the present Major [[Georg] Pausch, me, and Captain von Buttlar the task of remonstrating emphatically to the mentioned Major Scheel about his conduct, and use every means to change his ways. This was done, and because we saw it as the best means, offered him our friendship and association until he would find another way of life. However, he continued to perform the duty, which was miserable, during the time in the barracks.

I certainly spoke about this case with supposedly good friends, when questioned after our arrival in New York, but never thought that use would be made of it, to make anyone unhappy, who could have improved in the long run. After we were separated from our troops, all duty ceased of its own accord, and therefore it was impossible to refuse duty to the then Captain Scheel. Those assertions therefore, collapse and disappear, and the other point is also without basis, because if Major Scheel had not mentioned it himself, as often happens, expecting to find, from another quarter, his recall from Your Highness in New York, he would have held onto his position. Then, neither I, nor as I hope, any other officer of the 1st Battalion would have considered saying such an improper expression.

May Your Highness not take amiss my justification, which I am prepared to affirm under oath, if required, because with the most sincere devotion, I strive to be

    Bedford   Your Serene Highness
    7 May 1782   My most gracious Sovereign
                           And Lord's
                           Most humble servant,
                           F. von Germann

His Serene Highness, our gracious Prince, had the pleasure to name the previously Captain Scheel, of the corps under my command, major. Recently, after being assigned a short time, by me, he became so drunk, that he fell from his horse, lost his sword, and the watch had to carry him, nearly unconscious, into the hut of Lieutenant [Philipp] Schaeffer. Captain [Christian Ludwig], Count von Leiningen, [Christian Ludwig] von Schelm, and [Thylo] von Westerhagen, and Lieutenant [Jerome] Conradi publicly declared that Captain von Germann told them that the officers of the 1st Battalion refused duty with the present Major Scheel, because of his disgraceful conduct, and

Letters to the Prince

among other expressions, that if he did not obtain his release, they would drive him out of the battalion with sticks.

Sir, as the senior staff officer of the Hesse-Hanau here, I see myself obligated to mention this unpleasant situation, and, in so far as possible, to prevent evil consequences until it is reported to the highest level, and orders are received from there.

Awaiting your order in this affair, sir, I am with the most sincere devotion

Fort Knyphausen   Sir,
5 May 1782   Your most obedient servant,
                     Janecke

- - - - - - -

Sir, Most honored Lieutenant Colonel

Sir, I received your gracious letter of the fifth of this month, and it was very pleasant for me to receive the news of your continued good health from Lieutenant Conradi.

I am truly sorry that Maajor Scheel had the honor of reporting to you in a drunken condition. I have fully informed His Serene Highness, my gracious Prince and Lord, and given the gracious commission of major in your corps to this mentioned Major Scheel, and in the report of 30 April he has been removed from the 1st Battalion, and transferred to the Free Corps. The rest of what Count von Leiningen, von Schelm, and von Westerhagen, and Lieutenant

Letters to the Prince

Conradi, of your corps, have said about the remarks of Captain von Germann, of the 1st Battalion, I am not aware of, and the mentioned Captain von Germann apparently, upon questioning, must provide information about the subject, because the situation is completely unknown to me, and it is incorrect to cause a staff, or any other officer, misfortune. Therefore, I can add nothing except to submit my humble report, and a copy of your letter, to His Highness as His Highness has never written to me about your corps, except regarding the promotion of Major Scheel. As a result, I am not in a position to decide this or any other situation without receiving special orders from my gracious Prince.

Further, I have the honor to recommend myself most highly, and only desire the opportunity, under more pleasant circumstances, to show that I am always

Bedford on   Sir,
Long Island   Your most obedient servant,
6 May 1782   Lentz

- - - - - - -

Letters to the Prince

Most Illustrious Prince, Gracious Sovereign and Lord!

Your Highness, I lay the undersigned present lines in most sincere humbleness at your feet, and at the same time, request a gracious hearing from Your Highness.

As in the year 1776, all the officers, in exchange for the Brunswick military pay, most humbly joined Your Highness in the year 1780, they now most humbly sue for retention on the mentioned list, at a time when all necessities have risen to a completely exceptional price, which high price continues to the present. All the officers have suffered severe financial losses, and can no longer get by on their pay. Therefore, each one has the desire to improve his situation and at the same time, to be worthy at every opportunity of the proven benevolent favor and generosity, and to be worthy of a hearing at this time. After several previous gracious directives from the war commission, not only, but also in one dated 4 March 1782, it appeared to be Your Highness' pleasure to grant us the Brunswick military pay; now, according to a new most gracious directive dated Hanau, 18 July 1782, it has been determined that the vacancy monies and special benefits are to be completely taken away, and this will create a noticeably worse situation for all company chiefs and all the officers.

Therefore, we beseech Your Highness most

humbly, to inform us exactly what is meant by these special benefits, as we are fully convinced that it is not Your Highness' pleasure to reduce the previously agreed upon pay system.

We leave the matter to Your Highness' gracious disposition, and place ourselves most humbly in every situation, completely convinced by the benevolent character of our most serene Prince, that we can not put our fate in better hands than those of our most gracious Sovereign.

To whom we remain, in most sincere devotion until the last breath of our lives

    St. Antoine   Your Serene Highness
    19 June 1783   Our most gracious Sovereign
                            And Lord's
                            Most humble servants,
                            F. von Germann
                            F[riedrich] L[udwig] von Schoell
                            Von Buttlar

- - - - - - -

[The letter on pages 61 and 62 of the text in the Morristown National Historical Park Archives, written by F. von Germann and dated La Prairie, 4 September 1776, is in French and has not been translated.]

- - - - - - -

Letters to the Prince

Most Illustrious Landgrave, Gracious Hereditary Prince and Lord!

Your Highness, herewith I most humbly report that I was ordered to Canada by a general order, dated Charlottesville, 15 September 1779, to obtain uniforms there for the German Convention troops, and at the same time, as both Major Generals [William] Phillips and von Riedesel were going to New York on parole, on orders of His Excellency, Commanding General-in-Chief Sir Henry Clinton, I was ordered to proceed with their party and under the same parole.

Upon my arrival here, I found all the uniform items for the regiment in the royal storehouse. After properly reporting, the order was given that those items, along with other articles for the army, were to be sent to Virginia under a flag of truce. As soon as several cases were repaired, they were loaded aboard ship, and as I had received orders to remain here until further orders, Sergeant Knittel, of the Grenadier Company, who had come here from Canada with the baggage, was ordered to give special watch over the various items for the regiment by Lieutenant Farques, of the 20th Regiment, who has been ordered to Virginia.

I am also sending Your Highness, most humbly, a list of names of those from the regiment, as well as from the Artillery, who, in the few days that I have been here, I have been able to locate, and who for the most part have taken service in the Diemar Corps Private Halle, who previously served in Colonel [Andreas] Emmerich's Corps, which has now been deactivated, has joined me and been paid here. Drummer Gotz was also a non-commissioned officer previously with both of those commands.

As the Brunswick Major General von Riedesel reported to the mentioned Captain [Ernst Friedrich] von Diemar, that he would reclaim his troops during the coming year in order to send them to Canada, and he had willingly consented thereto. I have made the same suggestion concerning the Hesse-Hanau troops, whom he also promised not to retain, but to release, if so requested by Colonel von Gall. I will pay my respects to the colonel regarding this matter, if our situation permits. I must let this rest until another time, however, as it should not be expanded in an open letter. The troops are obtainable at any time, Your Highness.

It is to be assumed that both our major generals from Virginia were ordered here in order to arrange an exchange, and it is reported that such is actually being arranged, but I fear that we have little hope of any concrete results. Although all the American captives earnestly wish for a general exchange, the Congress appears to be set against it. Still, it is possible that, because of the recent expedition against Savannah, some softening of that position has developed.

Letters to the Prince

A detachment of about 7,000 to 8,000 men is ready to embark on the shortest notice. The commanding general, as well as Lord [Charles, Earl] Cornwallis, is to go with it, and His Excellency, Lieutenant General [Wilhelm] von Knyphausen is to take over the command of the army here. Apparently, this corps will undertake an expedition against a southern province. Your Highness, I will not neglect, most humbly, to report everything pertinent, which occurs during my stay here.

    In most sincere devotion, I strive to be

New York   Most Illustrious Landgrave
15 December 1779   Gracious Hereditary Prince
                            And Lord
                            Your Serene Highness'
                            Most humble, and truly
                            Obedient servant,
                            [Friedrich] von Geismar

- - - - - - -

    List of those members of the Hesse-Hanau Infantry Regiment Hereditary Prince, and the Artillery Company, who are presently in the army in New York

[A chart follows with the following headings: Name/ To which corps they belong/ Those who have served with the rebels/ Those actually in the Hussar Corps (Diemar's Corps)/ Those who have deserted. The chart contains the following information:]

    Sergeant Major [Johann] Moerschell, Artillery, in

Letters to the Prince

the corps as quartermaster

Free Corporal [Jacob] Haumann, Regiment, in the corps as sergeant, captured

[Heinrich] Faulstroh, Artillery, served with the rebels, in the corps as trumpeteer

Friedrich Alter, Regiment, served with the rebels, in the corps

Johann Braumann, Regiment, in the corps

Johann Iffland, Regiment, in the corps

Langhard, Regiment, served with the rebels, in the corps, deserted

Johann Ropp, Artillery, served with the rebels, in the corps, deserted

Johann Sentzell, Artillery, in the corps

Herinrich Schneider, Regiment, served with the rebels, in the corps

Lieutenant [Henrich] Siebert, Regiment, served as rebel lieutenant, in the corps as cororal

[End of chart]

Sergeant Knittel, detached from Canada

Bombardier Hestermann, detached from Canada

Drummer Gots, deserted in Virginia, and is now with the detached non-commissioned officers.

Musketeer Halle, had served with the Americans, but crossed the line, and took service with Lieutenant Colonel Emmerich. He is now with the detached non-commissioned officers.   [s] von Geismar

- - - - - - -

Letters to the Prince

Most Illustrious Landgrave, Gracious Hereditary Prince and Lord!

Your Highness, I have the pleasure herewith humbly to report that after I had sent the baggage from New York to Virginia this spring, the ransomed troops of the regiment to Canada, and had been exchanged by Major General Phillips, I went aboard ship for Europe, in accordance with my written orders. As soon as I had delivered my letters and dispatches from the generals to the minister, Lord George Germain, and His Majesty's First Adjutant, Lord Amherst, and laid myself at Your [sic] Majesty's feet, I will leave this place, in order to receive Your Highness' gracious orders. I will have the pleasure to deliver all lists and letters personally.

I have the pleasure in most sincere devotion, to strive to be

London
30 June 1780

Most Illustrious Landgrave
Gracious Hereditary Prince
And Lord
Your Serene Highness'
Most humble and obedient
Servant,
Geismar

- - - - - - -

Letters to the Prince

Order to Captain von Geismar, of the Hesse-Hanau Hereditary Prince Infantry Regiment

The request of Captain von Geismar, of the Hesse-Hanau Hereditary Prince Infantry Regiment, to be exchanged, and to go to Germany on leave, is herewith approved. However, as he was ordered by General Phillips to proceed to Canada to pick up new uniforms for the regiment and Artillery Company, it is necessary for the mentioned captain to carry out that order exactly. In as much as this general order can not be changed, should his exchange actually occur, and if General Phillips cancels the order so that Captain von Geismar is not to go to Canada, then he has permission herewith to return to the garrison in Hanau.

Given in North America, in Virginia, in Albemarle County, 18 September 1779
W. R. von Gall
Colonel and Commandant

Most Illustrious Hereditary Prince, Gracious Sovereign and Lord!

Your Highness, I most humbly lay myself at your feet, and present to you the accompanying general orders, which we have received, from the opening of this year's campaign to 19 July 1777, from General Burgoyne and Major General von Riedesel.

The situation in which we find ourselves, clearly

indicates the difficulties which must be tolerated in this barren region by everyone, in which there is no cultivated land to be seen in the surrounding twenty or thirty miles, and even less so an inhabitant, nor where the least common provisions for breakfast or supper can be purchased, so as to help sustain health and strength. Taking all this together, it is not too much to say, that one campaign here is comparable to three in Germany. It would be impossible for me to describe all the conditions which the soldiers here must tolerate, because the fatigue details on such poor and unhealthy rations are also very strenuous and must strike down the strongest individual. However, it is certainly an especially divine intersession that we have had so little illness, and no deaths in this campaign, as Your Highness will graciously see from this report.

In the hope of a gracious reception, I remain in the most sincere devotion

    In camp at   Your Serene Highness'
    Castleton   Most humble and obedient servant,
    21 July 1777   Ludwig Wilhelm von Passern

- - - - - - -

Most Illustrious Hereditary Prince, Gracious Sovereign and Lord!

As I do not doubt that Your Highness will have seen fit to give a gracious glance at the last package of general orders sent from here, I take this opportunity, once again, to lay the present included documents at your feet.

In part, Your Highness will see what our army has made in the way of marches and undertakings. The present situation is impossible to describe, because for some time we have remained behind the army, and must protect the provisions' magazines.

In most dedicated awe and respect, I strive with my last breath to be

    In camp at   Your Serene Highness'
    John's House   Most humble and truly
    28 August 1777   obedient servant
                        Ludwig von Passern

- - - - - - -

    Most Illustrious Prince, Gracious Sovereign
                and Lord!

Your Highness, herewith I send with most sincere humbleness a report about your regiment in Canada. You will have seen by the most humble report, which I sent in November last year, that the detachment was considerably strengthened by convalescents from the hospital, and now it has been strengthened by the baggage detail from Diamond Island, commanded by Lieutenant Seiffert, with three non-commissioned officers, and 27 privates, who joined me in December.

I venture to lay myself most humbly at Your Highness' feet, and to present a brief, most humble report about the condition of the detachment, and everything that has occurred since my last letter.

Letters to the Prince

All the troops of the detachment under my command are, thank Heavens, all healthy and well. They are adjusting to life at this place, and since being detached from the regiment, I have had no losses. Your Highness, I can most humbly assure you, that all the men have conducted themselves as becomes proper and honorable soldiers. I can also report to Your Highness, that with the concurrences of Lieutenant Colonel Creuzbourg, I have granted Musketeer [Peter] Bode of the Leib Company permission to marry the widow of a jaeger named [Johann] Eichel. I flatter myself that Your Highness will graciously approve, as I now have only three wives with the detachment, and the mentioned woman is a very industrious and good woman.

The events which have taken place since my last most humble letter to Your Highness are of no importance.

After being released at Fort Chambly, which has been occupied by 120 men, part Brunswickers, part my people, by the English, all the troops in Canada have marched into winter quarters. With the detachment, I occupied the parishes of St. Rose, St. Vincent, and St. Martin, on the Island Jesus, which lies about twelve miles from Your Highness' Jaeger Corps. I received orders on 26 January to unite the detachment with the mentioned Jaeger Corps, and to perform duty with it. We marched there together during very cold and bad weather, along the Chambly River to St. Antoine, where we halted and made camp. I finally camped in the parish of St. Denis, oppose St. Antoine. This march was the result of a movement by the rebels at Albany, who gave an indication of attacking us. However, because the route was so bad and the cold so severe, they could not carry it out. We broke camp here on 30 March, and marched into the parishes of Terre Bonne, La Chenaye, and Riviere du Chene, where the inhabitants had begun a rebellion, and so we were sent there to subdue them. At present I am in the parish of St. Eustache on the Riviere du Chene.

On 4 June we received letters from Cambridge, near Boston, where the captive German troops lie. They were brought by an adjutant of General Riedesel, by the name of Welow, [Willoe?] a captain in the English service, and all the equipment for Burgoyne's army is to be sent to Boston, and from there to the regiments. As no weapons are to be sent along, I made a trip to Three Rivers and personally separated them from the baggage. Colonel von Gall desired that Lieutenant Seiffert take the baggage to him, but that was not allowed by General [Guy] Carleton, because only one officer for all the German troops, and one non-commissioned officer per company, are allowed to accompany it. I have ordered Sergeant Knittel and Bombardier Hestermann on that detail.

Letters to the Prince

I assume Your Highness has more exact information from New England than we have here. That contained in the letters received during the latest opportunity amount to nothing, and everything from the rebels is false. Colonel von Gall is in Cambridge, and writes to me that they [the troops] are all well. Furthermore, I recommend myself and all the detachment to Your Highness' continued benevolence and favor, and especially recommend Sergeant Philipp Schaeffer, who up to the present time has performed the duty as sergerant major with untiring enthusiasm and diligence, so that nothing but this well-earned praise can be said.

I conduct drill currently three times per week, and have also begun shooting exercises. I have had the long, white summer overalls made for the troops, taking the money for them from the well-made beer for several months. They are very useful for the men. The old uniforms begin to be badly worn, and we look forward to receiving new ones.

As soon as the ships arrive from Europe, I will take the liberty, most humbly, to lay more, and more exact, information at Your Highness' feet.

I recommend myself to Your Highness' continued benevolence and favor, and strive with the most sincere respect to be

    St. Eustache   Your Serene Highness
    On Riviere   My most gracious Sovereign

Letters to the Prince

du Chene
23 June 1778

And Lord's
Most humble servant,
F. L. von Schoell

- - - - - - -

Most Illustrious Prince, Gracious Sovereign and Lord!

Your Highness, herewith I most humbly send a report of the detachment, and report most humbly that I was delivered the recruits by Captain Hense. These were seven non-commissioned officers, three drummers, and 93 privates. I also received complete uniform items: 96 shirts, 96 pairs of shoes, and 204 pairs of stockings for the detachment, from him.

I am in the greatest embarrassment because the recruits brought no uniforms or weapons with them, nor any for the rest of my detachment. The troops really need such items. I had long white overalls made for the recruits at once, in order to improve their situation, and wrote to General [Frederick] Haldimand requesting weapons from the English supply house, until such could be received from Germany.

Your Highness, I most humbly report also that because I have so few officers and non-commissioned officers for the presently very strong detachment, I have made four additional vice-corporals, whom I have put on the roster, and also given warrants as corporals, because the non-commissioned officers with the newly arrived recruits include many bad soldiers, have a very difficult duty, and because the troops are very widely dispersed. I hope Your Highness will accept this most graciously, and will most graciously send your orders as to how it can be handled in the future.

Together with the non-commissioned officers, I must watch that no excesses are committed, and that the detachment can maintain its previous good reputation. The newly arrived recruits will necessitate even more attention and effort to maintain discipline. However, I will spare no effort to maintain good order and discipline, and those who cause problems, will be severely punished Your Highness can be most humbly assured that I have had a heavy responsibility and work placed on me. The strong detachment, with so few officers and non-commissioned officers, and the thirty mile wide dispersal, creates much work. The necessity I have of picking up the necessary money every month in Montreal, the accounting with the commissariat for the provisions, handling the whole internal economy and accounting for the detachment, these things keep me busy day and night. I lie there now completely alone with 160 men, without having any officer with me, because Lieutenant [Ludwig] von Hohorst lies at Mascouche de Terre Bonne, which is more than fifteen miles from here, with fifty men; and Lieutenant Seiffert, together with Ensign [Friedrich Ludwig] Kempffer and 66 privates, has been detached to Three Rivers. That strong detachment and the considerable traveling which I must do, create large expenses, and Your Highness can not believe how everything has such an extraordinarily high price here.

I repeat, herewith, most humbly, to Your Highness that Surgeon Weiss requested of me, most humbly, to present the case for his release, to Your Highness, as he is inclined to seek his fortune here, in this land. Also, Grenadier Gruenewald requested that I most humbly ask Your Highness to allow him to remain here five or six years, when the troops leave Canada for Europe, so that he can work at his trade as an engraver, at which he can earn very much, here. Musketeer [Adam] Schwab of Captain Scheel's Company, born at Gainbach in Darmstadt, and married, has been unable to perform duty for a long time, and limps on the left foot, which he claims was injured by a batteau on Lake Champlain. I have had it examined, and all the surgeons assure me that it is an old injury. He is of almost no further use, as an invalid, and he has no great desire to remain here. Therefore, I await Your Highness' gracious order.

I would have most humbly sent Your Highness a rank list of the old detachment with this opportunity, if it had been possible to make one, but the troops are so widely scattered from one another, and the time was too short. As soon as I have the troops together again, which I have already requested of General

Haldimand, I will most humbly submit it to Your Highness. Your Highness' order that reports be sent as often as possible, will be punctually obeyed, and no opportunity will be allowed to pass without sending Your Highness reports about everything. Thank Heaven, all of the men of the detachment are healthy, but many of the recruits have the itch, which is a natural consequence of bad water and the ships' provisions, and which, when it is cured, makes the men very healthy and protects them against serious illness, as we of this regiment have learned from experience.

All information and news which I have about the regiment, I reported to Your Highness already in my most humbly transmitted letter at the start of May, which Your Highness will have received in a package from Lieutenant Colonel von Creuzbourg. Here in Canada everything is peaceful and the Canadians wait impatiently for the arrival of the French, which they fully expect.

I recommend myself also to Your Highness' benevolence and favor, and striver with the most humble respect, to be

Riviere du Chene Your Serene Highness
27 July 1778 My most gracious Sovereign
And Lord's
Most humble servant,
F. L. v. Schoell

Letters to the Prince

Most Illustrious Prince, Gracious
Sovereign and Lord!

Your Highness, herewith I most humbly transmit my report about the detachment. Since the last most humbly transmitted report to Your Highness, two recruits have died. The others are beginning to get sick. It is nothing of importance, but only the salted ships' rations and the change of climate.

I must also most humbly report to Your Highness that I have had to detach Lieutenant Seiffert with six non-commissioned officers and sixty privates to Three Rivers. General Haldimand ordered that they were to perform duty there as artillerists. I ordered 29 recently arrived artillery recruits, as well as two artillerists whom I had here in the detachment, and 29 men from the old detachment to go there. The general made arrangements with the 20 musketeers for a pay increase, so that they are to be paid the same as the artillerists from now on.

Your Highness, I must most humbly report at the same time, that Ensign Kempffer requested me to most humbly seek his release from Your Highness. He desires to seek his fortune in this country, and asks that his humble request be graciously granted.

We are still lying in cantonment quarters, but a few days ago received orders to be ready to march, but it only means a change of quarters.

I was in Montreal a few days ago, and while there

called upon General Haldimand. He received me very hospitably, and told me that he would visit me in the near future to observe the detachment at drill. I drill frequently with the entire detachment, and every other day with the recruits. Captain Hense brought sixty weapons with him from Portsmouth, which now are made at the King's expense, with a cylinder loading stock, and are to be given to the recruits to use. Now I am short of cartridge pouches and swords, because only cartridges came with the sixty weapons. The uniforms of the recruits are beginning to show much wear, and I do not know how I can start the winter in that condition.

Concerning the rebels, people here are quite at ease, although the general condition continues to improve the fortifications at Forts St. Jean and Chambly, and the defensive works at Quebec are to be improved and extended, also. General Haldimand has gone to St. Jean and is to return in eight days and muster us. Then we will learn our fate as to where we are to march. As soon as the general has been here, I will not neglect to give Your Highness all the news. Above all, I will not miss the opportunity, whenever it is possible, to send Your Highness a most humble report. Captain Hense will have the honor most humbly to give an oral report of our present camp, and the details of our situation to Your Highness.

I recommend myself now to Your Highness'

Letters to the Prince

continued benevolence and favor, and strive with the most sincere devotion and humble respect to be

    Riviere du Chene   Your Serene Highness
    6 September 1778   My gracious Sovereign
                                And Lord's
                                Most humble servant,
                                F. L. v. Schoell

P.S. Prior to his departure General Carleton issued the troops who marched last winter, every non-commissioned officer and private, a pair of shoes, a pair of gloves, and black cloth for winter breeches. I will try to have the black cloth exchanged for blue cloth.

        Most Illustrious Prince, Gracious
               Sovereign and Lord!

Your Highness, I have received your gracious letters of 3 February and 10 March. I will carry out the gracious orders contained therein most punctually with the most humble obedience. I have seen with painful regret, in Your Highness' gracious letters, that Your Highness has been displeased with me and believes that I have been disobedient, and acted in an insubordinate manner. I have learned about the military in a very hard school and know very well that obedience is the soul of the military, so that I would always support it. I have always striven to employ it strongly in practice, and call upon my superiors to

Letters to the Prince

bear witness if at any time I acted in the least otherwise. It is a misfortune for me that I have no opportunity now to be able to defend myself, but the fortunate moment will come again, and present itself when, with the most sincere devotion, I will have the sincere pleasure to explain the whole chain of events orally to Your Highness, and I know that my gracious Prince will allow me that gracious hearing. I therefore request my most illustrious Prince, most humbly, to cast no disfavor upon me, but only that Your Highness extend benevolence and favor to me. My most strenuous effort will only be directed to earning this high favor by my conduct, and to make myself worthy thereof.

    I now take the liberty of sending a most humble report to Your Highness, and to lay a most humble report at your feet, about everything that has occurred with the detachment since my last most humble letter to Your Highness.

    On 27 November 1778, the Drummer Schroeder, Grenadier Dephner, Musketeers Bauer, Haemerle, and Mueller attacked a resident in Petite Riviere du Chene at night, vigorously beat him and his wife, and according to their statements, planned to rob them, but did not take anything. This incident was reported to me the next morning, and I did all that I could, as the resident did not know the perpetrators. In order to find out who they were, I was fortunate enough to uncover the whole plot. The further consequences of the thing can be seen by Your Highness from the investigation and resulting court-martial, which Lieutenant Colonel von Creuzbourg will most humbly submit to you. The sentence was carried out completely on 24 and 29 February 1779, against the above noted five men who committed the act.

On 23 December 1778, I marched with the entire detachment into winter quarters on the Island Jesus, and entered the parishes of St. Martin, St. Francis, and St. Rose. The island lies ten miles beyond Montreal and is not one of the best quarters areas. On 23 January 1779, the recruit Caspar Weber, born at Ober Pimen, deserted. I caught him again on 23 June 1779 in Montreal, and he was punished by running the gauntlet ten times. On 3 August 1779, Free Corporal Busch and Corporal Orbig, as well as four musketeers, and three cannoneers, escaped from captivity here in the detachment. There was also a musketeer with them at Halifax, but soon thereafter was again captured by the von Seitz Regiment, which is quartered there, and with which he had served for a time. He was then sent here on the first departing ship, and was confined here at the detachment on 22 September 1779.

Letters to the Prince

On 16 July 1779 Cannoneer [Joseph] Elzer, who had lain dangerously ill in the hospital at St. Jean, deserted therefrom, and despite all efforts to find him, he could not be caught.   On 23 June 1779 Corporal Spahn, who was serving with the Artillery, was ordered to Niagara, with eight cannoneers. Grenadier Weitzel from the regiment, who had escaped from captivity, reported there and is still in Niagara, where he is to perform duty with Corporal Spahn until that detail is relieved, which General Haldimand has promised to do in the near future.

On 14 August 1779 Bauer and Pulfer robbed a resident in St. Rose, and as the resident reported it to Ensign Kempffer, commanding there, who then investigated the incident, Musketeer Pulfer deserted, but the next day was again seen in the region of St. Rose, in the woods, and as Musketeer Bauer believed that when Pulfer was recaptured, Pulfer would identify him, he made a plan with Musketeer Leonhard, born in Alsace, and with Muskeer Port, born at Eckenheim, and all three deserted. I tried everything, even sending out several patrols from the detachment and also several Canadians, who know the woods better than we do. The Canadians brought Musketeer Pulfer back in arrest on 18 August 1779. Musketeer Port, because he regretted deserting, returned voluntarily on 23 August 23 1779. Musketeer Bauer, who had planned to make his way to Albany, was captured by an

Letters to the Prince

English command lying at Yamaska, a parish about twelve and one-half miles below Sorel, and sent here in arrest. Musketeer Leonhard, who had separated from Musketeer Bauer after deserting, was recaptured again in Montreal, from which place I had him returned in arrest. Following that, Musketeers Bauer, Pulfer, Leonhard, and Port were sent to Lieutenant Colonel von Creuzbourg, and tried. The four musketeers were punished on 23 September, according to their sentence, as follows: Musketeer Bauer was punished by running the gauntlet, through the whole detachment, ten times, as a result, he was declared unfit to be taken into Hesse-Hanau military service again. Lieutenant Colonel Creuzbourg asked the general to take Bauer on a ship, which he promised to do. Musketeer Pulfer was punished by running the gauntlet eight times, and Musketeer Leonhard was punished by running the gauntlet five times. Musketeer Port, because he voluntarily returned, was punished with forty lashes, and Musketeer Werling with fifty lashes. All the deserters were then administered the oath again, and released from arrest. Musketeer Bauer, however, was not administered the oath, and is still in arrest.

I must also humbly report to Your Highness that Sergeant Heisterreich has been unfit for duty for nine months. He is quite lame on one side, and the local doctors think nothing will cure him but a mineral bath, which however, is not available here. Musketeer Wolf is also very sick, and as long as we have been in this country, he has had scurvy. He will have difficulty recovering therefrom. Musketeer [Johann] Wilhelm, who came with the recruits, has severe epilepsy, and can perform no duty as he often has attacks when on sentry duty. Therefore, I most humbly ask Your Highness if he may not be given his release., and he truly wishes to remain here and to enter a monastery here, where he will be well cared for as it is managed by the Catholic religion.

Cannoneer Merz froze his foot last winter, and the toes were amputated, so that he can no longer march.

Permit me, Your Highness, once again, most humbly, to recommend Sergeant Schaeffer to Your Highness' highest favor, as, since he has performed duty in the detachment as the sergeant major, he has always conducted himself with the greatest efficiency and devotion to duty. He will be a great loss to me.

Quartermster Sergeant [Henrich] Henzel lays himself most submissively at Your Highness' feet and has the absolute trust that our most illustrious and gracious Prince, who reaches out his benevolent and generous hand, even to the least of his subjects, will also show favor toward his four children, orphans since the death of his wife. He has previously carried out all his duties most eagerly, and I have been completely satisfied with his conduct. Quartermaster

Letters to the Prince

Sergeant Vaupel is to serve as sergeant major after the departure of Sergeant Schaeffer.

I received a letter from Colonel von Gall in the month of July, dated Cambridge, 15 October 1778, in which he sent me the new roster with Regimental Quartermaster [Carl August] Sartorious, and according to which I have paid the detachment to 8 October 1778. As according to the submitted roster, half of the forage and baggage allowances for the surgeons was to be withheld and credited to the treasury. I have done so. The surgeons, through me, most humbly request that your Highness graciously authorize the full payment of the forage money. Colonel von Gall ordered me to publish the promotion of five men to private first class: Grenadier Freund, Jr., Musketeer Ewald of the Leib Company, Musketeer [Adam] Amand, of the Colonel's Company, Musketeer Mieckel, of the Major's Company, and Musketeer [Andreas] Ungar, Sr., of Captain Scheel's Company.

Sergeant Knittel and Bombardier Hestermann have not yet returned and we have no further information about them.

May I dare, Your Highness, to burden you with a most humble request, which is that Your Highness graciously order to have sent here in the coming year, someone with uniform items for the detachment's officers, because we can not get epaulets, hat trim, sword knots, and such items, which we are completely

Letters to the Prince

out of.

I still have not dared, most humbly, to introduce my present situation to Your Highness, and to request most humbly for relief, but the firm trust which I have in the known generosity and benevolence extended so graciously to all those who have the honor to be in Your Highness' service, by Your Highness, make me confident, to represent to Your Highness, most humbly, that as I currently command a very large detachment, and therefore find it necessary to have many expenses, which I can not reduce, I therefore venture to request a small allowance with the most submissive humbleness. I nervously write this and most humbly ask that even if Your Highness should not approve my most humble request, that I find no disfavor from you, and you may be absolutely certain, that in any event, that at all times I remain the truest and most humble servant of my most illustrious Prince, and will direct all my efforts at all times through dedication to duty and proper conduct to earning the favor of my gracious Prince, and making myself worthy of such.

I received the order on 12 September to be prepared to march with the entire detachment to Quebec. The Anhalt-Zerbst Regiment has been there until now, and it is said that I am to relieve it.

The entire detachment is, thank God, still healthy, except for those listed in the report, and the troops have become fully accustomed to the climate. As the enemy gives us nothing to do, I do not neglect to earnestly drill, and as often as possible, to conduct sham exercises at the exercise area. I have drilled the entire detachment twice weekly throughout the summer, but unfortunately, the entire detachment is not uniformly armed.

As I have been ordered by Lieutenant Colonel von Creuzbourg to submit an invalid list, I have complied, and in accordance, named Cannoneer Merz as such. He is to depart for Europe with Sergeant Schaeffer.

Quartermaster Sergeant Henzel gave me a most humbly written request for Your Highness, with the request that it most humbly be laid at Your Highness' feet. Therefore, I take the liberty most humbly, to forward it. I have just received the orders to send Musketeer Beier to Quebec with Sergeant Schaeffer. He will go there with him.

I gave Sergeant Schaeffer forty guineas from the military chest to take with him, for which he must make a proper accounting upon his arrival in Hanau, and which is to be used to defray the travel expenses for himself and the invalids.

Your Highness, I most humbly submit herewith a report, and a rank list for the detachment.

I also take the liberty to recommend myself and the entire detachment to Your Highness' favor and grace.

Letters to the Prince

I lay myself most humbly at Your Highness' feet, and remain with the most sincere respect and humble submissiveness

   St. Martin   Your Serene Highness
   9 October 1779   My most gracious Sovereign
                      And Lord's
                      Most humble servant,
                      F. L. v. Schoell

Most Illustrious Prince, Gracious Sovereign and Lord!

Your Highness, herewith I lay a report in most sincere humbleness at your feet.

As I have just heard in General Haldimand's anteroom, from his adjutant, that an express is leaving here in half an hour for Halifax, I do not wish to let this opportunity pass without most humbly sending Your Highness a most humble report and information.

On 16 October, I received the order to march to Quebec with the detachment. I set out on 27 October, and arrived here safely with the entire detachment on 4 November, and at once marched into the barracks with music playing. The non-commissioned officers and privates are very comfortable in the barracks, but we officers must lodge in the city, which hits us very hard, as for bad quarters I must pay ten piasters, but receive only three piasters a month. We perform duty here with the 31st Regiment, which serves five days and I serve three days, on watches. For this, 1 captain-of-the-day, 1 officer, 13 non-commissioned officers, 1 drummer, and 94 privates are needed. The duty is very demanding for the officers, and I have the duty three days in every week, but it is better that the men are kept together, so they can be more closely observed, and kept in order. General Haldimand, at my request, has promised that the Artillery, as well as the musketeers, ordered thereto, who are under the command of Lieutenant Seiffert, and assigned in St. Jean, Sorel, Isle aux Noix, and Niagara, are to be ordered back here at an early date, so they can perform artillery duty here. This will be a great relief for me, because these many detachments make an astonishing amount of work for me, in keeping accounts.

I also report most humbly to Your Highness, that since the departure of Sergeant Schaeffer, nothing new has taken place in the detachment. The men are, thank God, all healthy and well and satisfied. General Haldimand delivered, free to all the troops in Canada, for each man, a wool blanket for an overcoat, a pair of winter breeches, a pair of shoes, a pair of shoe soles, and a pair of gloves.

In the near future, General Haldimand is to observe the drill and exercises of the detachment. All the generals and staff officers of the army, now in Canada, can not give praise enough for the good appearance made by the troops, and the uniforms of the detachment. Whenever I hold guard mount, an astonishing number of people rush to the parade ground, and I must give credit to the entire detachment that they exert every effort during drill, and also in their conduct.

I will also most humbly obey, as promptly as possible, Your Highness' most gracious orders sent to me, and allow no opportunity to pass for sending Your Highness a most humble report.

I recommend myself and the entire detachment to Your Highness' further favor and grace, and strive with the most profound respect and most sincere submissiveness to be

Quebec
7 November 1779

Your Serene Highness
My most gracious Prince
And Lord's
Most humble servant,
F. L. v. Schoell

- - - - - - -

Most Illustrious Landgrave, Gracious
Sovereign and Lord!

Your Highness, herewith I send, in most sincere humbleness, a report on Your Highness' regiment, which I command.

During the month of August, I most humbly transmitted a report, and a rank list to Your Highness, but as the letters go very uncertainly, therefore, I again send in most sincere submissiveness a report concerning everything which has occurred in the detachment since the departure of Sergeant Schaeffer.

Although we passionately await letters and news from Europe, nevertheless this year, we have not yet received a line. Therefore, I take the liberty of repeating that which was reported most humbly in all the letters I sent Your Highness last year, and offer it again in this letter, in most sincere submission.

The whole detachment, except for a few sick individuals, thank God, is well and satisfied. During the month of July the detachment was mustered by the English muster commissary, Major Holland. Lieutenant Colonel von Creuzbourg will most humbly send the list to Your Highness, as I sent the list to him so that he could do so.

On 3 October, I led the detachment in shooting exercises and maneuvers for General Haldimand, which earned his special satisfaction. A large number of English, and all the Hessian officers were present. A small maneuver, which I made with the detachment, came at the end.

May I risk a most humble request be laid at Your Highness' feet on behalf of Free Corporal Busch and Corporals [Johannes] Orth and [Georg] Becker. Although those men have committed serious offenses, it was done more from excesses of youth, than as a sign of evil. Furthermore, they all claim a true and proper regret, and have demonstrated a proper change since then. I venture also most humbly to recommend Sergeants Vaupel and Hensel, as well as Quartermaster Sergeant [Adam] Kohlep, to Your Highness' continued favor. I and all the officers lay ourselves most humbly at Your Highness' feet, and ask that we be allowed to continue to enjoy Your Highness' benevolence and favor, and be assured that all of us would sacrifice body and soul with the greatest pleasure for our gracious Prince.

Surgeon [Wilhelm] Schuetten has requested his release, and at the same time, desired to sent a letter to Your Highness. I could not convince him to do otherwise. Above all, he is a young, ill-bred, and obstinate individual who understands very little about his profession, but is still defiant. He has done very little in the detachment except shaving beards.

We will not enter winter quarters before 10 November, although it already freezes very hard, because work on the fortifications is being pushed very hard. The detachment is to go fifty miles below Quebec in the parishes of Islette, St. Ignace, and Port

Jolly, or St. Jean, and in the brigade of the Brunswick Lieutenant Colonel [Ernst] von Speth. Lieutenant Colonel von Creuzbourg with his corps, is to enter the brigade of the brigadier, Colonel von Rauschenplat, of Anhalt-Zerbst service, and the winter quarters are to be sixty miles above Quebec, so that I will be 110 English miles from him.

I repeat again, most humbly, all that which I laid at Your Highness' feet in my last letter, and recommend myself and the entire detachment to Your Highness' continued benevolence and favor.

With the most sincere submissiveness, I strive to be

In camp on the	Your Serene Highness'
Plain of Abraham	Most humble servant,
23 October 1780	F. L. v. Schoell

Maneuver

The detachment marched from the left, out of the camp, to the plain lying in front of the camp. Here the detachment wheeled, bringing the right to the front again, and awaited the general, who passed the front. The detachment then marched, in sections, past the general-in-chief, in parade formation, and wheeled upon coming to its first position, so as to make the front from the left.

Next, there was a charge from that place, twice by platoons and twice by the entire detachment, then twice advancing and twice in retreat. The detachment then marched from the right, taking a half distance, and the sections formed a division, closed to deploy, and then deployed from the left. It then marched forward to where a bridge had been set up, charged the bridge four times by platoons, and passed the bridge with the middle platoons firing constantly. On the opposite side of the bridge, the detachment formed an open square. Twice platoons charged from the square, and several times with an entire flank. The detachment then marched off, by files, to form a front. This was followed by an attack and then a retreat back to the bridge, which was crossed while taking a constant fire from both wings. This side of the bridge was charged twice more by platoons, followed by the detachment marching to the rear, in four columns, for a predetermined distance, at which point the detachment again wheeled to the left.

Then followed a march from the right, by platoons, and the maneuver to cover an artillery train or baggage was made. The 1st platoon led, the 2nd, 4th and 6th platoons wheeled to the right, and formed the right flank. The 3rd 5th and 7th platoons formed the left flank, and the 8th platoon closed the formation. This oblong, open formation then marched, and when it halted, "Form a front!" was commanded. It charged forward before forming the detachment again with platoons in column. Then, as it was assumed the enemy had met the head of the column, it was necessary to win space to maneuver.

Platoons marched toward the middle, and the maneuver came to an end.

Most humble Report of those Changes, which have occurred in the Detachment from the Time when Sergeant Schaeffer departed until the present Date

On 26 October 1779, I received the order to march to Quebec with the detachment. I marched there from St. Martin on 27 October, after drawing the detachment together from St. Francois and St. Rose. From Montreal, where I obtained bateaux, I continued my journey, unhindered, by water to Quebec, where I arrived on 4 November, and with the detachment was quartered in the barracks there. The 31st Regiment and the detachment constituted the garrison.

On 27 December, Lieutenant Seiffert, who had been detached to St. Jean with the Artillery, prior to this time, joined us here in Quebec, and the non-commissioned officers and privates, who had been on command, rejoined the detachment, and those who were actually artillerists did service with the English Artillery.

On 2 March 1780, Cannoneers Reif, [Johann] Jahn, and [Johann] Handel were arrested because they sought to be engaged by an English non-commissioned recruiting officer. An investigation was held and they were punished by running the gauntlet, according to the sentence by Lieutenant Colonel von Creuzbourg.

On 11 March, it was reported to me by Corporal Kohlep that Musketeer Leick had told him that Corporal Buss tried to get him to desert when the mentioned Leick was about to lie down to sleep. I investigated the situation at once, and after getting further information, arrested Free Corporal Buss at once. After contacting the auditor of the Jaeger Corps and investigating further, I found that Corporals Orth and Becker, and Musketeers [Philipp] Menck and [Peter] Fix were also implicated. I sent Lieutenant Colonel von Creuzbourg the results of the investigation, from which Your Highness will be sent an extract, as all investigations conducted by the detachment have been most graciously sent to him. Lieutenant Colonel von Creuzbourg directed those arrested to receive the following sentences: Corporals Buss, Orth, and Becker were permanently reduced in grade, and the first to run the gauntlet on two days, twelve times each day; Corporal Orth to run the gauntlet on two days, eight times each day; and Becker to run the gauntlet on two days, six times each day, through the entire detachment. Musketeers Menck and Fix however, to be punished by running the gauntlet on one day, This pronounced sentence was fully carried out against the five arrestees.

As Lieutenant Colonel von Creuzbourg approved the promotions of Quartermaster Sergeant Vaupel to sergeant, and Corporal Kohlep to quartermaster sergeant, I announced those promotions to the detachment on 24 May 1780. Both these non-commissioned officers have conducted themselves well in the detachment, and performed duty especially well.

On 26 June, ships arrived from New York, bringing Free Corporal Haumann and fourteen musketeers and one drummer; Bombardiers Moerschel and Hestermann and three cannoneers, and two drummers from the Artillery. All had ransomed themselves [from captivity]. Among the musketeers, two arrestees by the names of Schenot and Huffner were included, because while in New York, they had again deserted from Captain von Schlagenteufel of the Brunswick troops, who commanded all the troops assembled in New York, and tried to enlist in an English free corps. After an investigation, the two musketeers mentioned were punished according to the sentence by Lieutenant Colonel von Creuzbourg, by running the gauntlet.

Two companies of the Hesse-Cassel von Knyphausen Regiment and three companies of the von Lossberg Regiment came with the ships from New York. Other companies of the two regiments are partly in captivity, and partly lost in a storm on a previous voyage coming here. Colonel [Johann] von Loos and Colonel [Henrich Christian] von Borck arrived with them. The first received a brigade immediately after arriving here, in which I am assigned with the detachment, and he formed a combined battalion from the five companies of the two regiments.

On 2 July, Grenadier [Johann] Weitzel arrived at the detachment. He had ransomed himself and arrived here after a long and difficult trip by way of Oswego.

On 23 July, Musketeers [Georg] Freyensoehner and [August] Velden of Colonel von Gall's Company, arrived here. They deserted from the rebels at Fort Stanwix and arrived here after a difficult and tiring trip, under constant pursuit by Indians serving the rebels, naked and bare, and with close-cropped hair, because the Indians had cut off all their hair. On 26 July the Artillery moved about a mile out of the city and entered camp there. I gave them the presently surplus, old tents and field items, to take with them.

On 24 August, the entire garrison lying here moved into camp about half a mile outside Quebec. As we had no tents, they were delivered to us from the English magazine. Here in camp, called the Heights of Abraham, are the 31st and 44th Regiments, the Hesse-Hanau detachment, the Hesse-Cassel combined battalion, and two Brunswick companies. We were required to supply very strong commands from the camp, for the Quebec fortifications.

On 2 October, Musketeer Weber deserted from the camp, and despite all efforts, he has still not been caught. However, he can not possibly avoid capture, and will certainly soon be caught. This is the second time he has deserted.

As in many incidents, the requirement of sending a

provost from another corps has created very great expenses, therefore, Lieutenant Colonel von Creuzbourg consented to the request that Drummer [Samuel] Otto of the detachment, who had volunteered, should perform the duty of provost. This Drummer Otto is furthermore small, can not play, and even if he could, he has no drum.

On 6 October, Cannoneer Reif deserted from the Artillery camp at St. Michel, but a few days later he was brought back by a command of Brunswickers. After an investigation, it was the sentence by Lieutenant Colonel von Creuzbourg that he be punished by running the gauntlet.

Lieutenant Colonel von Creuzbourg promoted Quartermaster Sergeant Henzel, after his having been recommended by me, to sergeant. I flatter myself that the promotion will meet Your Highness' most gracious approval, as the mentioned quartermaster sergeant has had the honor to serve the illustrious house of Hesse-Hanau for a long time, and while he has been with the detachment, has conducted himself exceptionally well, and performed his duty diligently.

As Corporals Buss, Orth, and Becker were demoted as part of their sentences, [the detachment] lost three non-commissioned officers. Therefore, with the concurrence of Lieutenant Colonel von Creuzbourg, the Musketeers [Georg Carl] Ungar, Storck, and Brust were made vice-corporals, and as additional inducement, were paid the vacant corporals' pay. I flatter myself that this will please Your Highness, as I have had so few non-commissioned officers in the detachment.

I have sent no non-commissioned officers to Europe this year, as I have received no such order from Your Highness.

I recommend myself again, all the officers, and the entire detachment to Your Highness' continued favor and grace, and strive in most sincere submissiveness to be

In camp on the	Your Serene Highness'
Plains of Abraham	Most humble servant,
23 October 1780	F. L. v. Schoell

P.S. Sergeant Knittel, who was ordered to take the baggage from here to the regiment, delivered it and returned to New York with Bombardier Hestermann, but when the baggage and uniform items arrived in New York, the mentioned Sergeant Knittel was ordered to deliver the uniform items from there, to the regiment in Virginia.

Letters to the Prince

Most Illustrious Landgrave,
Gracious Prince and Lord!

I received Your Highness' most gracious letter of 19 March 1780 on 17 December 1781. Filled with gratitude, I lay my most humbly thanks at Your Highness' feet for the most graciously granted monthly allowance. I will strive most strenuously by an ever-increasing dedication to duty, and untiring diligence to make myself worthy of the favor of my most illustrious and gracious Prince.

Your Highness, I lay a most humble report and information about everything that has occurred since my last forwarded report at Your Highness' feet.

The entire detachment is in the best condition, only a complete issue of weapons is missing, which I still have not been able to obtain from the English stores despite my best efforts, because the arming of several newly raised corps has left them empty. I have kept the weapons of seven individuals most graciously ordered back to Europe, in order to arm those newly arrived. I flatter myself that Your Highness will graciously approve of this. May I once again, presume humbly, to seek permission from Your Highness for the release of Surgeon Weiss, as since the arrival of Regimental Surgeon Heidelbach, his loss could be tolerated easily.

As several Negroes came with the fleet from New York, I have temporarily taken on two as drummers, and await Your Highness' orders if more such can be used in the detachment.

Vice-Corporals Brust, Storck, and Ungar have been paid as corporals by me, as the result of the demotion of Corporals Buss, Becker, and Orth, and as the duty in Quebec in the previous year, and also while in winter quarters, because the houses were widely scattered in the parishes, was very difficult, I have allowed Musketeers [Jacob] Tack and Foerster to serve the regiment as vice-corporals with lance corporal pay. I flatter myself that Your Highness will accept this all the more graciously, since these individuals have conducted themselves especially well.

General Haldimand was surprised and satisfied by last year's maneuvers, which were held in his presence, and especially as many young non-commissioned officers commanded their platoons during the maneuvers with the greatest attention to detail and accuracy. Above all, I must recommend all the officers and most of the non-commissioned officers that I have the honor to command, for their exceptional efforts at every opportunity to show their dedication to duty, and the welfare of the detachment entrusted to me. I venture most humbly, therefore, to recommend them to Your Highness' continued favor.

We are still in camp although the weather is very cold, and it appears we will not enter winter quarters before the first of November. Where the detachment is to be, I do not yet know, and we will not know until General Haldimand, who has gone to Montreal, returns, and we are still to have maneuvers before that.

At least everything is undisturbed by the enemy and fortunately still as peaceful as in the previous year. However, there are rumors spreading that the French commanding general in America has won the Iroquios Indians over to his side with gifts, and they are to attack here in Canada, over Niagara. But all of this needs confirmation, and if it were to take place, they would be received warmly enough, as our army is once again quite strong and in the best condition. The Hesse-Cassel von Knyphausen Regiment has been ordered back to New York from here, and has actually already departed.

I and all the officers, as well as the whole detachment, lay ourselves most humbly at Your Highness' feet and recommend ourselves to your continued benevolence and favor.

I strive in most sincere submissiveness to be

In camp near Quebec

Your Serene Highness
My most gracious Prince
And Lord's
Most humble servant,
F. L. v. Schoell

- - - - - - -

Letters to the Prince

Most Humble Report
Of that which has occurred in the Detachment Since the previous Year's most humbly submitted Report

On 9 November the detachment moved out of the camp near Quebec and marched into winter quarters in the parishes of St. Anne, Grondines, Dechambault, and Cape Sante, which constitutes a district of 36 English miles. These parishes lie between Three Rivers and Quebec, and are the best in the whole province. They were originally intended for the Hesse-Hanau Jaeger Corps, but General Haldimand ordered a change shortly before the troops broke camp, and ordered me to enter these quarters.

On 28 November Cannoneer Reif was punished by running the gauntlet according to the sentence by Lieutenant Colonel von Creuzbourg, for desertion.

On 5 March part of the detachment was mustered by the English muster commissary, Major Holland, at Cape Sante and Dechambault; on the 6th at Grondines, and on the 7th at St. Anne. The muster list is most humbly enclosed herewith.

On 20 April Musketeer Kuehn, because he wounded his hostess with a musket shot, was arrested and locked up for a long time. The investigation of this incident was submitted to Lieutenant Colonel von Creuzbourg, who will must humbly submit more details. The arrestee is still confined, and Lieutenant

Letters to the Prince

Colonel von Creuzbourg has still not ordered anything else. The individual has a serious and melancholy temperament, and everything indicates that he committed the act while feeling extremely melancholy. He had never quarreled with his host family, and had never previously demonstrated an evil heart, nor a malicious character. The wounded woman had fully recovered after four weeks, as the wound was not serious.

On 5 August I ordered the whole regiment to St. Anne, and again, on 6 August it was mustered by Major Holland, as noted in the accompanying muster list.

On 16 September the recruits from Hanau, escorted by Lieutenant Thoma, arrived. Those officers, non-commissioned officers, and privates of the regiment, named on the accompanying list, arrived here.

On 19 September I marched with the detachment out of cantonment quarters and entered the camp at Quebec, where on the morning of the 21st, and later in the day, I delivered to Captain Pausch those artillerists who had been under my command. The mentioned Captain Pausch requested a surgeon from me. Therefore, I gave Sergeant Weiss to the Artillery, pending further gracious and more definite orders.

F. L. v. Schoell

- - - - - - -

Letters to the Prince

Most Illustrious Landgrave,
Gracious Prince and Lord!

Your Highness, I most humbly report herewith that although the package was already closed and aboard ship, ready to go, Musketeer Joachim Mueller was sent here from the hospital as an invalid. I was unable therefore to send the required invalid list therein.

Captain-at-arms [Adam] Kirchoff, ordered to Europe, received forty pounds sterling to help him on his trip.

I recommend myself again to Your Highness' benevolence and favor, and strive most submissively to be

    Quebec   Your Serene Highness'
    21 October 1781   Most humble servant,
                                      F. L. v. Schoell

Most Illustrious Prince,
Gracious Sovereign and Lord!

Your Highness, I most humbly report herewith that Colonel Lentz arrived here, fortunately, on 6 October with the exchanged officers of the 1st Battalion. I learned from him that Your Highness had most graciously given me the Vacant Company, resulting from Captain Scheel's promotion to major, for which in most sincere submissiveness I most humbly thank Your Highness. This new favor from my illustrious Prince will encourage me even more, and make it my eternal duty to sacrifice my body and property with pleasure, in the service of such a gracious Prince. All my efforts and my whole being is dedicated only to the service of Your Highness, and I will consider myself the most fortunate of men if I can make myself worthy of my illustrious and gracious Prince by my steadfast dedication to duty and diligence.

My most humbly submitted report and information from the start of the previous month to Your Highness will have already been received by now.

Sergeant Heisterreich returns to Europe as an invalid this year. This individual has caused me a great amount of vexation due to his evil and malicious character. He is thoroughly evil.

My family situation makes it necessary for me to present a most humble request to Your Highness, which consists thereof, that in the coming year, after the end of the campaign, if everything remains the same as at present, and we do not have to anticipate an attack during the winter, that I be graciously allowed to depart from here for Europe with the fall fleet, and after a two month stay, at the earliest order from Your Highness to return to the battalion, and await Your Highness' further gracious orders. Please forgive me, most illustrious Prince, that I dare to bother Your Highness, with this most humble request Only the benevolence and favor with which Your Highness has

Letters to the Prince

honored me at all times, and the good fortune I have had to serve3 Your Highness, allow me to risk this letter, and I would be the most wretched individual if thereby I should cause Your Highness displeasure.

Your Highness, allow me in closing most humbly to recommend myself to Your Highness' continued benevolence and favor, and again ask a gracious approval of my most humble request.

I remain to the last breathe of my life, in most sincere submissiveness

    In camp at   Your Serene Highness
    Point Levi   My most gracious Prince
    19 October 1782   And Lord's
                               Most humble servant,
                               F.L. v. Schoell

- - - - - - -

Most Illustrious Hereditary Prince,
Gracious Sovereign and Lord!

As Captain von Buttlar has remained behind, sick in the barracks at Albemarle, I have the great honor to submit this report on the Leib Company to Your Highness. It suffered the following losses from 30 January 1781 to and including 10 April.

Private Wilhelm Grimm, who rejoined the company as a prisoner of war, deserted from the barracks at Albemarle on 7 February. Private Johannes Weitzel, who had leave from the company until 12 February, did not report back. On 20

February we received orders from Colonel Wood to march at once to Winchester, and as there were not sufficient wagons available, most of our sick and our baggage had to be left behind. Privates [Conrad] Krieg and [Caspar] Kempf were detailed to guard it. The two hautboists [Adam] Mueller and Insdorf, Jr., who upon request to the commanding officer, Colonel [James] Wood, had leave [to work] on the land, remained behind at the barracks in Albemarle. Also, Hautboist [Georg] Insdorf, Sr., and Private [Johannes] Hallatschka remains behind sick. The company had not a single man sick, nor a deserter during the entire march from the barracks to Winchester, nor during the three weeks, when the regiment lay at the warm springs. However, while there we received orders again to march to Lancaster in Pennsylvania. We had already reached the border of Maryland, when we again received the unhappy order from Congress to return to Winchester. During this march, on 5 April, Privates Caspar Kohlep and Carl Lentz deserted from the camp near Martinsburg, and Privates Peter Stein and Philipp Mahr deserted from the bivouac near Winchester on 10 April.

    During the morning of 11 April, the order from Congress was made to us that our men were to be separated from us, and we were to have no further command over them, and actually the same afternoon, they were taken from us, to a barracks four miles from

Letters to the Prince

Winchester by a detail. How disturbing and painful this moment was for all the officers, can be more easily understood than explained. To the present time, no officer has been allowed to visit our troops in the barracks. However, I hope it will soon be permitted. Still, our men are not closely confined, and we see some of them every day. Even though I am separated from the company at this place, I will not neglect my responsibility toward every man in the company, and my greatest pleasure is to do everything in my power to help them.

God grant, that we are soon exchanged, and that is our wish day and night.

I strive with the most sincere devotion to be, and remain in all humbleness

My most gracious Prince's
Most humble and truly obedient servant,
Von Eschwege

- - - - - - -

Most Illustrious Hereditary Prince,
Gracious Sovereign and Lord!

As Your Highness has been graciously been pleased to promote me to staff captain in the Leib Company of the Hesse-Hanau 1st Battalion, I must express my sincere thanks to Your Highness for this great honor. I also thank Your Highness most humbly for the yearly allowance of 250 Gulden, which Your Highness has granted me as staff captain of the Leib

Letters to the Prince

Company.

I will never forget this most gracious testimony. In the future I will always strive to exactly follow all orders given to me, so that I may earn the future most benevolent approval of my dearest Prince.

Your Highness receives herewith a report on the officers and privates who are in Your Highness' Leib Company here. I strive with the most sincere appreciation and respectful sentiment to be

New York
7 May 1782

Your Serene Highness
My most gracious Prince
And Lord's
Most humble and obedient
Servant,
Staff Captain von Eschwege

- - - - - - -

Most Illustrious Hereditary Prince,
Gracious Sovereign and Lord!

I have the pleasure to submit a report about the Leib Company, of the detachment which is here, to Your Highness. Since the last report of 7 May 1782, which I had the pleasure to send to Your Highness, nothing else of consequence has occurred, except that the Hautboist Insdorf, Sr., arrived here from Philadelphia on 8 May with a flag of truce, and once again joined Your Highness' Company. The Americans released him because of his age, without asking for anyone in exchange. It is especially

Letters to the Prince

disappointing to report that there is no hope of having our men, who are still in captivity, exchanged. According to the latest reports, which Colonel Lentz has received from Pennsylvania, the Musketeer Heinrich Koehler has rejoined the company.

We have awaited the order to embark for four weeks, in order to sail to Canada. However, one week follows another, and the best season for a fleet to go to Canada has arrived, so I do not know what that means. A few days ago the news arrived here that a French fleet of thirteen to sixteen ships-of-the-line are cruising outside the harbor at New York. This could certainly cause some hindrance, and be the reason that we have had to remain here this month.

I strive with the most sincere respect to be, and remain

Governors Your Serene Highness
On Long Island My most gracious Prince's
4 August 1782 Most humble and obedient
  Servant
  Staff Captain von Eschwege

- - - - - - -

Most Illustrious Hereditary Prince,
Gracious Sovereign and Lord!

Letters to the Prince

Most Illustrious Hereditary Prince,
Gracious Sovereign and Lord!

Your Highness, I have the pleasure, most humbly to report that I have been ordered by my colonel, Lentz, to remain here in New York to provide money, and when possible, uniform items to the captives of the 1st Battalion, who are still in Reading [PA], and some in Philadelphia, in Pennsylvania, and after they are exchanged, to take them to Canada. To accomplish this I have received an instruction from my colonel, which I, to the best of my ability, will strive to follow. My colonel has also ordered me, most humbly to report that, as the passage between here and Canada is too difficult and slow, and as he therefore can not send orders to me from Canada, I should turn most humbly to Your Highness, and await all further orders as long as I am here, from Your Highness.

The company left twelve uniforms here for me, which I am to give to those who ransom themselves. However, should all of those men, who are now in captivity in Reading be exchanged, I will find myself in a very embarrassing situation as to how to clothe those people, as absolutely no uniforms were left with me for them. May Your Highness have the grace to order how I should handle that situation.

A commission has again met in Jersey in order to

work anew on a prisoner exchange. How far they have gone, I am unable to learn.

Your Highness, I must also most humbly report that Hautboist Insdorf, Sr., who suddenly fell ill, died here in the hospital on 20 August. The colonel left Drummer [Wilhelm] Giese behind with me here. The fleet for Canada, on which the officers of the 1st Battalion are, sailed from here on the second, or third of this month. Your Highness, I must in truth admit that it made me very sad to be ordered to remain behind here in New York, as I had looked forward to Canada for a long time. Although I have the pleasure of commanding Your Highness' Company, I must be the only officer from the battalion who remains here. However, as that can not be changed, I only wish from the bottom of my heart, that the prisoner exchange would take place soon, so that I might be in condition to rejoin the regiment in the coming year.

I strive with the most sincerely respectful sentiments to be, and remain

New York
7 September 1782

Your Serene Highness
My most gracious Prince's
Most humble servant,
Christian von Eschwege
Staff Captain

- - - - - - -

Letters to the Prince

Most Illustrious Hereditary Prince,
Gracious Sovereign and Lord!

Your Highness, I had the great pleasure in my last report dated 7 September 1782, most humbly to report that I was ordered to remain behind in New York by my Colonel Lentz, to await the exchange of prisoners from the lst Battalion who are still in Pennsylvania. I also mostly humbly reported to Your Highness that a commission had met to work on the exchange of prisoners. However, I have still heard nothing as to what they decided. I fear, however, that there are very many difficulties to overcome for this exchange.

As, since I command here, no one from the lst Battalion has ransomed himself, and as no flag of truce has sailed to Philadelphia, I have still not received the latest news about our captives. At the earliest opportunity I will write to the sergeant majors requesting that they send me a name list of all those men who are still in Reading.

The recruit transport, which arrived some time ago in Halifax, is expected here daily. Concerning the fleet with which the lst Battalion officers sailed from here, I have heard nothing since the time of their departure. I hope however, that they have had a good trip as the entire month of September was unusual, being without a severe storm, and the English fleet, consisting of 26 ships-of-the-line, was cruising along the coast, and safeguarded their journey.

Letters to the Prince

    I strive with the most sincerely respectful sentiment to be, and remain
        New York   Your Serene Highness
        1 October 1782   My most gracious Prince's
                                      Most humble Servant,
                                      Christian von Eschwege
                                      Staff Captain

- - - - - - -

        Most Illustrious Hereditary Prince,
        Gracious Sovereign and Lord!

    Your Highness, I have the great pleasure most humbly to report that nothing developed again this year concerning the prisoner exchange, and it appears also likely that nothing will come of it in the next year.

    I have spoken with Lieutenant Colonel Kempel, who is responsible for the exchange negotiations, and was a member of the last commission. He told me there could be no hope for an early exchange.

    First, the Americans want to negotiate as the Free United States, and second, they demand an exorbitant amount of money. As it appears the exchange is not at hand, therefore I proposed to Lieutenant Colonel Kempel that it would be very beneficial to send winter blankets to our captives, as they have received none for such a long time, and also offered to be helpful to him in the matter. This he promised me, but did not believe there were as many blankets available now as all the captives would need. However, a great many were expected from England with the next fleet, and as soon as they arrive, he would propose it to the commanding general, Sir Guy Carleton. As soon as I have received these blankets, I will obtain a pass in order to deliver them to the troops, myself, with a cartel ship. However, if I am refused the pass, because last year the Americans would not allow a captain to go there, then the commanding Brunswick officer, who is now a Lieutenant Reinecke, since the captain recently died, will take care of it. In general, we will see to it that all those things which we wish to send to our men in the future are arranged in turn, so that the Duke of Brunswick's captives, who are in the same barracks with ours in Reading, receive the same as ours receive. This was noted in the instructions given to me by my colonel, according to which, I will eagerly strive at all times. Still, not a man from the 1st Battalion has ransomed himself out of captivity. A jaeger by the name of August Neuberger of Colonel von Creuzbourg's Corps arrived here from Philadelphia on a cartel ship exchange. I will care for him here, and send him to Canada at the first opportunity, in the spring.

According to the latest news from Halifax, it is assumed that the recruits will not come here this winter. Concerning the fleet on which the officers of the 1st Battalion sailed to Canada, I have still not heard the least news.

Letters to the Prince

I strive with the most sincerely respectful sentiment to be, and remain

New York
20 October 1782

Your Serene Highness
My most gracious Prince's
Most humble servant,
Christian von Eschwege
Staff Captain

- - - - - - -

Most Illustrious Hereditary Prince,
Gracious Sovereign and Lord!

Your Highness, I have the great pleasure most humbly to report that on 5 December, one surgeon, seven non-commissioned officers, and one private, and today, 15 December 1782, another seven privates of the 1st Battalion and the Artillery, ransomed themselves out of captivity. The names of all these men may be seen by Your Highness in the list which I am sending to Your Highness, as well as those others still in captivity, and where they come from, which you may be pleased to see.

Your Highness will be surprised to see in the list that so many men have taken service with the Americans, and still others have indentured themselves, but the Americans have applied cruel methods to force the men to do that. First, Congress sent the captives written addresses, in which they were informed that they had been completely forgotten by their King, and by their princes, and that they had no

Letters to the Prince

hope of being exchanged. As a minimum compensation for their long confinement, Congress asked 80 Spanish dollars for each man, and then he can have his freedom and settle in the country as a free citizen. Those who can not pay the 80 dollars, should find a farmer, who will pay for them, and as a repayment, they are to work as servants for three years. The other choice is to become a soldier, as most are encouraged to do, and they have been promised many things. The sergeant majors brought two copies of the address which was read to them every day. I have had it copied word for word, and send it to Your Highness herewith.

Your Highness will be able to see what terrible lies the soldiers have been told. Those who refuse to take service, and who do not sell themselves as servants, are thrown into jail and threatened to take service every day.

I have reported this cruel treatment, not only to Lieutenant General [Friedrich Wilhelm] von Lossberg, but also to the commander-in-chief, Lieutenant General Carleton. Lieutenant General Carleton immediately sent a protest concerning this to General [George] Washington.

The seven men who arrived today had taken service in a regiment which was called the Congress Regiment, but had taken service with the intent, at the earliest opportunity, to redeem themselves here in

Letters to the Prince

New York. They assured me that still other men of the 1st Battalion have taken service with this regiment, and await the opportunity to come here. These men, and also the non-commissioned officers who came from Reading, were brought through by well-intended farmers. I have myself spoken to these farmers and told them they should bring more of our men here. This they promised me. Therefore, I hope to receive more men soon.

Some of the 1st Battalion took service on an American warship, and planned to free themselves at the earliest opportunity. Only Corporal [Peter] Weber and Private Kohlep of Your Highness' Leib Company had taken such service. Most have sold themselves as servants, and the others still sit in captivity. I fear that those who sold themselves as servants will have the least opportunity to get away, because their masters will always keep a very close watch over them.

The men who have come in here are all shabby. As I have only twelve uniforms available, I see the necessity of buying cloth in order to clothe the men. They have all had to tolerate a great deal on their marches, especially Sergeant Major Vaupel and Surgeon [Wilhelm] Gottschalk, neither of whom could walk well, but still had to make difficult marches. They could only travel at night, and had to avoid all main roads. Lieutenant General von Lossberg sent a regimental quartermaster to the captives, with whom I

Letters to the Prince

also sent to those members of the 1st Battalion and the Artillery, who are still in prison, money, blankets, and brown cloth for long breeches, which was a gift from the King. Furthermore, Lieutenant General von Lossberg has been very kind and has promised me help in every situation.

I received a letter from my colonel in Quebec, in which I saw that all the officers of the 1st Battalion arrived safely on 6 October 1782. A packet of letters from Your Highness to my colonel also arrived here recently. I have them in safe keeping, and as there are no ships to Canada at this time, I will not be able to forward them until next spring.

Your Highness, I now request most humbly that as the orders given to me by my colonel were to remain here until a general exchange, and as there is no prospect of such an exchange, I most humbly ask Your Highness to grant me permission to travel to Canada next summer with the men who have ransomed themselves, or that I be relieved by another officer. My desire to return to the regiment, and my long absence therefrom, force me to this most submissive presentation.

I await Your Highness' most gracious order concerning this with the greatest humility, and strive with the most sincerely respectful sentiment, to be

New York   Your Serene Highness
15 December 1782   My most gracious Prince's

Letters to the Prince

> Most humble servant,
> Christian von Eschwege
> Staff Captain

- - - - - - -

Most Illustrious Hereditary Prince,
Gracious Sovereign and Lord!

Your Highness, I had the greatest pleasure, in my last report, to mention that some men of the 1st Battalion, who had been in captivity, had taken service on an American warship. Now I have the pleasure to inform Your Higthness that the frigate, on which the men took service, and which had the name *South Carolina*, was captured by the English and brought safely into this place. After a thorough invetigtion, 29 men of the 1st Battalion and one man of the Artillery were found thereon. I reported this at once to the commander-in-chief, Sir Guy Carleton, who with the concurrence of Admiral [Robert] Digby, had these men, who had already been taken to the guard ship, with the other prisoners, brought here. All the men were individually questioned by a Hesse-Cassel auditor, concerning their opinion of duty on the ship.

However, their statements were all the same, they had been taken captive and were forced either to pay 80 Spanish dollars or take service, and on the advice of many well-intentioned individuals, who were loyal to the King, they took service on the ship, because they had been told that this ship certainly would be captured immediately by the English, as soon as it entered the ocean, because there were reports that an English ship was cruising in the area, giving special attention to this ship. Or, if that failed, their contract on the ship was that they only had to serve six months, and after that time they could go wherever they wished, and then they would try to return to their regiment. Therefore, they were all released and given over to my responsibility.

The month of December 1782 was also a very good month for the regimernt and the Artillery, because with the 22 men who had ransomed themselves, when I already had the pleasure of mentioning it in my last most humble report to Your Highness, another 52 men returned this month. None of the men are performing any duty, as I still have received no weapons for them. Their old uniforms have been patched, as best as possible, and they have been issued small clothing items. Lieutenant General von Lossberg told me that the commander-in-chief, Sir Guy Carleton, had promised to send the men to Canada as soon as possible, and I will direct all my efforts to insure that it takes place at the earliest time. Major General [Carl Wilhelm] von Hachenburg, in whose brigade I have the honor to serve, is very kind and does everything possible to provide the best care for my men.

The thirty men who were taken from the ship,

have been given nothing more than one Spanish dollar, each, against their pay credits, because I do not know if it would please my colonel if I paid out everything owed to them. But since the day they came from the ship, they now receive their full pay.

From Your Highness' Leib Company there was not a single man on this ship, and I am sorry to mentoion to Your Highness that most of the men from the company have contracted with the farmers for two or three years, which time must be fulfilled, and I fear that it will be difficult even then to get them away. According to the information which I could get about the men, some of them have already married.

I strive with the most sincerely respectful sentiment to be, and remain

    Brooklyn   Your Serene Highness
    On Long Island   My most gracious Prince's
    14 January 1783   Most humble servant,
                         Christian von Eschwege
                         Staff Captain

Letters to the Prince

Most Illustrious Hereditary Prince,
Gracious Sovereign and Lord!

Your Highness, I have the great pleasure most humbly to mention that since my last report, dated 14 January 1783, nothing of importance has occurred in my detachment, except that a grenadier private, Lorentz Vetter, who ransomed himself out of captivity, has reported in. He had also taken service in the American Congress Regiment for a short time, but has now rejoined here.

A few days ago my detachment was armed, and the weapons were delivered from the English magazine. However, I have made the reservation that these weapons, either here or in Canada, are to be returned as soon as they are no longer used.

The Brunswick detachment is under my command, and has duty together with mine. It is especially pleasant for me, that my men, as regards uniforms, have again reached a point where they can all report for duty. Although their uniforms are not new, I have exchanged or mended all, and they look quite good again, and all this has been accomplished at very little expense. I drill them every day, and believe it is necessary, as they have not been active for such a long time.

Above all, I am very satisfied with all my men, and I have not the least complaint with any one of them. Also, there has been no illness. As within a short time, a fleet is to sail from here to Newfoundland, and I already have a list of those men of my detachment, which I must send to the regiment in Canada to give to the commander-in-chief, therefore, I assume that it is his wish to send my men with the fleet as far as Halifax, as the passage to Canada is still not open.

The Hesse-Cassel regimental quartermaster, who went to Pennsylvania in order to provide the captives with money, has still not returned. Therefore, I am still not in a position to give Your Highness detailed information about the present condition of the remaining captives of the 1st Battalion.

I strive with the most sincerely respectful sentiment to be, and remain

    Long Island   Your Serene Highness
    7 March 1783   My most gracious Prince's
                                Most humble servant,
                                Christian von Eschwege
                                Staff Captain

- - - - - - -

    Most Illustrious Hereditary Prince,
      Gracious Sovereign and Lord!

Your Highness, I have the great pleasure, most humbly to report that since my last report of 7 March, nothing of significance has taken place in the detachment.

The order which I received about four weeks ago,

Letters to the Prince

that the Brunswick and Hesse-Hanau detachments were to be prepared to sail to Nova Scotia has not been canceled, and I hear that the time of embarkation is to be about the fifteenth of this month However, as there are now many rumors circulating about peace, and the commanding general awaits confirmation by the next packet boat from England, this departure could be delayed, and possibly even canceled. The final destination of both these detachments is Port Roseway in Nova Scotia, to which place a large number of refugees are traveling in order to settle there, and these are to be accompanied by the two detachments. His Excellency, Lieutenant General Sir Guy Carleton, has promised that both detachments are to remain there for only a few weeks, and are then to be sent to Canada.

Some of our men are beginning to become sick, but it does not appear to be a dangerous illness. The rash is especially on the hands. Meanwhile, I must give Surgeon Gottschalk credit that he is doing everything possible to control this illness. Therefore, I hope that it will soon be overcome.

A few days ago I received a letter from Regimental Quartermaster [Ludwig] Flachshaar, of the Hesse-Cassel troops, who went to Pennsylvania already in December 1782 to take money and uniform items to the captives. In the letter from Lancaster, dated 27 February, he wrote to me that he had encountered from the 1st Battalion, one non-commissioned officer, five hautboists, and three privates in Philadelphia; one non-commissioned officer and 27 privates in Lancaster; one surgeon, three non-commissioned officers, and 38 privates in Reading; and seven privates in Friedrich and Yorktown. He had also, now and then, met quite a number of men from the 1st Battalion with farmers in the countryside. However, he had not given them any money, but only consoled them about an exchange. These are the men noted in the list, which I had the pleasure of sending to Your Highness last December, who had indentured themselves to the farmers. However, if an exchange should occur, I hope that many of the men will return. He did not send me a list of all of these men. Therefore, I am not in a position to send Your Highness a report about them.

 I strive with the most sincerely respectful sentiment to be, and remain

  Long Island   Your Serene Highness
  4 April 1783   My most gracious Prince's
          Most humble servant,
          Christian von Eschwege
          Staff Captain

- - - - - - -

Letters to the Prince

Most Illustrious Hereditary Prince,
Gracious Sovereign and Lord!

Your Highness, I have the great pleasure, most humbly, to report that on 15 April, I received the order, late in the evening, that the Hesse-Hanau and Brunswick detachments were to embark the next morning, on 16 April. In the present situation the order was completely unexpected, as I firmly believed that I would keep these troops here until the captives, who were all awaited here in the very near future, had arrived, since the peace had been settled. They would then have completed a shipment, and I could have taken all of them to the regiment in Canada at the same time. However, both detachments were the first ones sent from here to Halifax. As a few Brunswick officers went along, they also had the Hesse-Hanau detachment under their command, as far as Halifax. There, officers of Your Highness' troops are available, and they will take the detachment under their command, and, I assume, arrange for the voyage to Canada as soon as possible. With this fleet I sent seven non-commissioned officers, one surgeon, one drummer, and forty privates, and gave Sergeant Major Vaupel all the accounts concerning them. It is especially pleasant for me to send such good non-commissioned officers, on whom I can rely completely, with them.

About eight weeks ago I received orders from

headquarters that both detachments were first to go from here to Port Roseway, but the latest order was that they were to go directly to Halifax. I hope their stay at that place is not a long one, as the passage to Canada is now open.

Since my last report to Your Highness, dated 4 April, six men of the 1st Battalion, who had taken service in the American Congress Regiment, have returned here. Three of them arrived here on 23 April, and, as the fleet was already lying in the harbor, it was too late to send them with it.

I have held back five non-commissioned officers and three privates of the 1st Battalion, and one non-commissioned officer assigned the Artillery. As only a few non-commissioned officers remain with the other captives, I considered it best to keep one from each company here, except for the Grenadier Company, none of which were here.

All the prisoners from the army are to be assembled at a designated place in Pennsylvania or New Jersey, and yesterday I received the order from headquarters to be prepared to march to that place in a few days, to receive the captives from the 1st Battalion and the Artillery.

I strive with the most sincerely respectful sentiment to be

    Walllabout   Your Serene Highness
    On Long Island   My most gracious Prince's

Letters to the Prince

27 April 1783 Most humble servant,
Christian von Eschwege
Staff Captain

- - - - - - -

Most Illustrious Hereditary Prince,
Gracious Sovereign and Lord!

Your Highness, I had the greatest pleasure in my last report, dated 27 April, most humbly to mention that I had received the order from the commanding general, Sir Guy Carleton, to send the Hesse-Hanau detachment and also that of the Duke of Brunswick, under my command, to Halifax at once, and for me to be prepared, personally, to travel inland to receive the remaining 1st Battalion and Artillery captives, and to bring them here to New York to be exchanged. I began my journey on 1 May, and together with other officers of the army, under the command of Brigadier General [Alfred] Clarke, went from here to Philadelphia to await the resolution of Congress about the exchange. Upon our arrival, it became obvious that all the difficulties had been resolved, and the prisoners who were in Philadelphia received the order to march to New York at once. I found one non-commissioned officer, and four hautboists of the 1st Battalion and three privates of the Artillery there, whom I sent away with the first shipment. I then received permission to go to Lancaster and Reading to assemble our prisoners at those places. However, it

Letters to the Prince

turned out that they had already been ordered to march to New York several days previously. I met them, already underway, and discovered that the Hesse-Hanau and Brunswick troops had marched in a division from Lancaster and Reading.

In the division were a surgeon, three non-commissioned officers, and fifty privates of the 1st Battalion, and four privates of the Artillery. I escorted all of these men safely over to Staten Island, where they lay a few days, and then were loaded directly onto a transport ship. I received the order immediately to embark the other troops lying on Staten Island, and, according to my orders, I was then to take all these men to Canada.

Since 13 May I lie on the ship, and during this time, more of the men of the regiment have returned. I hope, at least, still other men who are scattered about in the countryside will return. It will surely be difficult for those who have indentured themselves to farmers for a fixed number of years, to get away. However, I hear that Congress has sent an order to the farmers that all such men are to be released. It may possibly be another fourteen days before I leave from here, and during that time, I hope that more will return.

Of Your Highness' Leib Company, I have sixteen privates here. I have reports of five or six who will surely return, if it is possible, since they have indentured themselves. However, the others have told their comrades, who have returned, that they have no desire to return to Germany, and that they wish to seek their fortune in America. Among this number, the most definite are Musketeers Koehler, [Conrad] Orth, Wald, and Stein, who have told their comrades they wish to remain in this country. Concerning [Daniel] Rueffer, Wiskemann, [Conrad] Traut, and Maul, and several others, I still have the hope that if they can get away from their farmers, they will return to the company.

Shortly before my arrival in Philadelphia, Hautboist [Adam] Mueller died of an apoplectic stroke. The other hautboists are all here. I have purchased a few new uniforms here at a very cheap price, and given them to a few of those who no longer had any. All of them have received such small clothing items as were needed. I have received money enough here to pay out all the amounts for which the men have credits. However, as I have [no] company books here, and do not know exactly what is owed each one, I have paid each one something on account, and will return the remaining money to the regiment. If, after my departure, some men of the regiment arrive here, Lieutenant General von Lossberg has been so kind as to promise to take care of those men, and to send them to Canada at the earliest opportunity. Furthermore, Lieutenant General von Lossberg has

Letters to the Prince

shown much goodwill toward me and my men during my stay at this place.

A corporal of the Jaeger Corps by the name of [Eckhard] Nentzel, who was captured near Albany, also arrived here after being exchanged.

Whether I am to stop at Halifax, is still unknown to me prior to my departure from here, so I will again ask at headquarters that the detachment which I sent from here, be sent to Canada as quickly as possible.

I strive with the most sincerely respectful sentiment to be

    Transport ship   Your Serene Highness
    Joseph at   My most gracious Prince's
    New York   Most humble servant,
    23 May 1783   Christian von Eschwege
                               Staff Captain

Letters to the Prince

Most Illustrious Hereditary Prince,
Gracious Sovereign and Lord!

I had the pleasure to receive Your Highness' most gracious letters of 12 and 26 March, on 2 June.

Your Highness ordered me most graciously therein that I should not neglect helping the exchange of the 1st Battalion prisoners, and upon their arrival here, should either take them to Canada, or directly to Hanau. Your Highness may rest assured that I will spare no effort, since I obtained permission to go to Philadelphia in order to get all the prisoners of the 1st Battalion and the Artillery released, that I possibly could, of those who sat in prison and in huts, and to bring them back here, personally. However, as so many men had indentured themselves, and as they have not yet been released by Congress, the number of privates of the 1st Battalion has not been as numerous as I wished. Everything possible has been done by the commanding general, Sir Guy Carleton, and Lieutenant General von Lossberg, to get those men released, and Brigadier General Clarke is in Philadelphia for that purpose, but so far it has been to no avail.

Two privates of Your Highness' Leib Company, of the 1st Battalion, by the names of Rueffer and [Nicolaus] Pohl, who had indentured themselves, got away from their farmers and arrived here safely on 24 May. From my report dated 23 May, Your Highness

Letters to the Prince

will have seen how many men I personally brought here from captivity. I lie here together with all those people on board the transport ship, and daily await the order, either to sail to Canada or directly to England. However, it appears that the commanding general still has not decided where I am to sail.

The debarkation of the 1st Battalion, which I had to send from here to Halifax, debarked there and entered the barracks. I hope Ensign von Gall, who is still there, will provided the best of care for those men.

I strive with the most sincerely respectful sentiment, to be

On the transport ship *Mary*
3 June 1783

Your Serene Highness
My most gracious Prince's
Most humble servant,
Christian von Eschwege
Staff Captain

- - - - - - -

Most Illustrious Hereditary Prince,
Gracious Sovereign and Lord!

Your Highness, I have the great pleasure, most humbly to report, that I received the order on 21 June 1783 from headquarters, to sail immediately, with the detachment under my command, to England, and to halt here at The Downs, where I was to await further instructional orders from Lord North, First Secretary of State of His Majesty, after my having sent a report to him.

Letters to the Prince

After a voyage of forty days, I arrived here at The Downs, 31 July, without having lost a man during the crossing, and wrote to Lord North immediately, according to my orders, and requested further instructions from him. I await his answer hourly. Except for the ship, named *John and Bella*, only two others, with Brunswick troops, sailed together from New York, and fortunately have also arrived here. Otherwise, I have not encountered any Hesse-Cassel or Hesse-Hanau troops here.

About five days before my departure from New York, I received confirmed information from headquarters that the detachment under my command was no longer to go to Canada, but directly to England. As this detachment still was without weapons, and I did not know if I could obtain weapons in England, or anywhere else during my voyage to Hanau, I asked His Excellency, Lieutenant General von Lossberg, to help me with such. His Excellency had not the least difficulty in delivering the necessary weapons for my detachment from the Hesse-Cassel magazine, and ordered me to report it most humbly to Your Highness immediately upon my arrival here. Since my last report to Your Highness, dated 3 June, more men of the 1st Battalion have returned to duty. Four of them arrived at the last moment prior to the ship's sailing, and therefore could not be provided with weapons. A Grenadier

Letters to the Prince

Schlingellof deserted from the ship at New York on 5 June 1783, and went inland again.

As to what will now happen to the indentured men of the 1st Battalion and the Artillery, I am sorry to report to Your Highness, that the efforts of Brigadier General Clarke have not gone as well as was expected, because very few men have come back. In an effort by Hesse-Cassel to do as much as possible, Major [Carl Leopold] von [sic] Baurmeister of the Young Lossberg Regiment was sent to Philadelphia, also, to do as much as possible to obtain their release. It is true that many of those indentured men have no desire to rejoin the regiment, but there are some among them who have a strong desire to return to their fatherland. Lieutenant General von Lossberg has had the kindness to insure me that if the men of the 1st Battalion, or the Artillery, return to New York, he will care for them just as well as for the Hesse-Cassel troops.

I strive with the most sincerely respectful sentiment to be, and remain

Downs
31 July 1783

Your Serene Highness
My most gracious Prince
And Lord's
Most humble servant,
Christian von Eschwege
Staff Captain

Most Illustrious Hereditary Prince,

Letters to the Prince

Gracious Sovereign and Lord!

Your Highness, I had the pleasure in my last report from The Downs, dated 31 July 1783, most humbly to report that I had arrived safely in England from New York with the detachment under my command, and that hourly I awaited the orders from Lord North, after having reported my arrival to him.

On 2 August, I received an answer from Lord North, who informed me that I was to proceed to Bremerlehe at once, and then travel onward to the place of my final destination. However, as a few days later, three companies of the Hesse-Hanau Free Corps arrived at this place from New York, I was therefore detained not only a few days longer, but was sent aboard ship with those three companies, making the troops very cramped. However, we had a fortunate trip and arrived at Bremerlehe on 22 August without having lost a man.

On the 23rd I and the detachment under my command landed and entered quite good quarters at once. The 24th and 25th were rest days, and on the 26th we continued onward with our trip. The local official, who traveled as march commissary with us to Witzenhausen, laid out the march route that far, for us, which I have the great pleasure to send herewith to Your Highness. Upon my arrival here, I was offered money for expenses, and to pay the detachment under my command by a local merchant, on orders of the

Hesse-Cassel agent who lives in Bremen. However, as I had been supplied with sufficient funds to pay the detachment until we reached Hanau, I did not take any. In addition to this money, I still have 500 pounds sterling in bank notes, in the military chest. The three companies of the Hesse-Hanau Free Corps have received no pay for August, and have no opportunity of getting money here. Captain [Jost Friedrich] von Francke is therefore very embarrassed, and requested that I help him financially. Therefore, I have already advanced him something for the August pay.

With the payment for the non-commissioned officers and privates of the detachment, I have managed until now, according to the pay instructions of the 1st Battalion and the Artillery as it was done in America, and will continue to do so, without making any changes until I receive Your Highness' most gracious orders about it.

I strive with the most sincerely respectful sentiment, to be

Bremerlehe
24 August 1783

Your Serene Highness
My most gracious Prince's,
Most humble servant,
Christian von Eschwege
Staff Captain

- - - - - - -

Letter to the Prince

MARCH ROUTE

For the Hesse-Hanau detachment, consisting of 1 officer, 13 non-commissioned officers, 9 drummers, and 76 soldiers, a total of 99 men, and the other three companies, from Bremerlehe to Witzenhausen

Day	August	
1st	24	- in Geestendorf and Wolsdorf County Vieland
2nd	25	- Day of rest
3rd	26	- Dannen Hagen
4th	27	- Ritterhude, Noble Court of the von der Licht and Wersebe
5th	28	- Day of rest
6th	29	- Arbergen Goh, Court of Achim, crossing the Wuemme at Borgfeld
7th	30	- City of Verden
8th	31	- Day of rest
	September	
9th	1	- Hemsen, County Woelpe, crossing the Aller at Verden
10th	2	- Stoecken, County Neustadt
11th	3	- Brelingen, County Biessendorf, crossing the Leine at Stoecken
12th	4	- Day of rest
13th	5	- Linden, Court of Linden
14th	6	- Adensen in County Calenberg

Letter to the Prince

15th	7	- Daensen and Limmer, Noble Court of Bock and Kamecke
16th	8	- Day of rest
17th	9	- City of Einbeck
18th	10	- City of Nordheim
19th	11	- Weende, County Harste
20th	12	- Day of rest
21st	13	- Friedland and Luetgen Schneen, County Friedland
22nd	14	- Witzenhausen on the Werra, Hessian territory

Hannover
9 August 1783

d'Estorff
Quartermaster General
Copied by v. Reiche

- - - - - - - -

Most Illustrious Hereditary Prince,
Gracious Sovereign and Lord

Your Highness, I have the great pleasure, most humbly to report, that, according to my march route, I arrived at Witzenhausen on the Werra, on 14 September, with the detachment under my command.

During the entire march through Electoral Hannover, there was not the least complaint about a single man of my command. Also, on the other hand, my men were very much pleased by the hospitality of the inhabitants. However, I am sorry to have to mention to Your Highness, that in the last night in

Letter to the Prince

quarters at Friedland, Musketeers [Henrich] Fischer and [Georg] Mahr, Sr., quarreled and each wounded the other. Musketeer Mahr is dangerously wounded, having received two cuts in the head. Because of this danger, I have allowed him to be questioned by a Hesse-Cassel official here in Witzenhausen. Musketeer Fischer is only lightly wounded, and I have placed him in arrest. As far as it is in my power, I will provide the best care for the dangerously wounded Mahr, and have the surgeon apply all his skill for a recovery. Further, I will spare no effort maintaining the best discipline in my command, while passing through Hesse-Cassel, and try to prevent all excesses.

I strive with the most sincerely respectful sentiment to be

Witzenhausen
14 September 1783

Your Serene Highness
My most gracious Prince's
Most humble servant,
Christian von Eschwege
Staff Captain

Most Illustrious Hereditary Prince,
Gracious Sovereign and Lord !

Your Highness, I have the great pleasure most humbly to report that today, 24 September, I arrived here at Nauheim with my command.

Letter to the Prince

On the entire march through the territory of Hesse-Cassel not the least disorder occurred, and not a single complaint was lodged with me at any of our night quarters. The wounded Musketeer Mahr is progressing quite well, and I have not failed to have the surgeon give him the best care. I still hold Musketeer Fisher under arrest.

I will march away from here tomorrow morning at seven o'clock and, according to my march route prescribed by Your Highness, will arrive in Hanau tomorrow.

I strive with the most sincerely respectful sentiment to be

Nauheim   Your Serene Highness
24 September 1783   My most gracious Prince's
                        Most humble servant,
                        Christian von Eschwege
                        Staff Captain

Letters to the Prince

Most Illustrious Hereditary Prince,
Gracious Sovereign and Lord!

As Your Highness has had the kindness to promote me to 1st Lieutenant, and to transfer me to the Leib Company of the Hereditary Prince 1st Battalion, I see it as my duty and responsibility to express my most humble thanks to Your Highness, and to recommend myself to Your Highness' continued favor.

With the same opportunity, I wish most humbly to report that because of the absence of Staff Captain von Eschwege, and with the concurrence of Colonel Lentz, I have taken over command of Your Highness' Leib Company, about which I have the pleasure to submit a report herewith, and to mention to Your Highness that the following three musketeers have been transferred to Your Highness' Leib Company: Phillipp Traut, born at Windecken, 32 years old, 5' 9 ½" tall; Wilhelm Breidenbach, born at Rockenheim, 33 years old, 5' 8 ¾" tall; and Friedrich Meyer, born at Goebingen, 30 years old, 5' 5 ½" tall. The first two were from Captain Schoell's Company, and the latter from Colonel Lentz' Company.

I strive with the most sincere respect to be, and remain

In camp at Your Serene Highness, My most
Point Levi gracious Prince and Lord's
16 October 1782 Most humble servant,
[Carl] von Lindau

Letters to the Prince

Most Illustrious Hereditary Prince,
Gracious Sovereign and Lord!

I do not want to miss the opportunity with the presently departing packet, most humbly, to send Your Highness a report concerning the Leib Company of the Hereditary Prince 1st Battalion, and to add the changes therein, which have taken place since my last mort humbly submitted report of 16 October, from the camp at Point Levi, namely: Sergeant Major Vaupel, Quartermaster Sergeant Lenz, and Musketeer Remmy ransomed themselves at New York, as Your Highness will graciously see in the accompanying report. In a letter which I received a few days ago from Ensign von Gall, from Halifax, I received the news that they, and the other men of the 1st Battalion who had ransomed themselves, reported there on 5 May. Your Highness, I most humbly must report that Musketeer Georg Tempell, born at Altheim, 5'11¼" tall, returned here to the Leib Company on 28 May. The mentioned Musketeer Tempell was left behind because of illness when the Burgoyne army retreated on 8 October 1777, and he fell into enemy hands. Thereafter, he sat for a long time in the jail at Albany, but was finally released. From there he made his way to the Indians, and fortunately arrived at Niagara, where he had to take service with Butler's Rangers, a royal provincial corps. After surviving two years, he finally received his discharge, and permission to return to the 1st Battalion.

I must also report, most humbly, that Surgeon Gottschalk left the Leib Company on 14 March 1782, and went to Your Highness' Jaeger Corps as regimental surgeon.

I strive with the most sincere respect to be, and have the pleasure to remain for life, with the most humble submission

    In winter quarters   Your Serene Highness
    At Lotbiniere   My most gracious Prince
    15 June 1783   And Lord's
                        Most humble servant,
                        von Lindau

Most Illustrious Hereditary Prince,
Gracious Sovereign and Lord!

Your Highness, I have the pleasure, most humbly, to submit a report about Your Highness' Leib Company of the 1st Battalion, and to add those changes which have occurred since my last most humbly submitted report of 15 June, from the winter quarters at Lotbiniere. Regimental Drummer [Leonhard] Klee returned to service in New York on 28 April 1783. Four other hautboists, by the names of [Johannes] Andre, [Christoph] Insdorf, [Johannes] Raab, and Emmert, as well as 18 privates, were exchanged on 12th and 24th of May, as Your Highness will have the pleasure to see in the accompanying report, and such captives go about in New York as ordered. I must also most humbly report to Your Highness, that the previously Musketeer [Friedrich] Weingarten has been promoted to corporal, and Hautboist Adam Mueller, born at Steinau, 45 years old, died in May in Philadelphia. I must also most humbly report, that Corporals [Johannes] Bellinger and Tack, as well as 23 privates, went as ordered, to Quebec on 29 June, to work on the fortifications there. The company, which is not strong, has grown weaker because of the departure of these work details, and presently consists of only 15 privates. Since the 25th of this month we are in cantonment quarters at Point Levi, and apparently are to embark in three or four weeks on the ships coming here, and then sail to Europe, where all of us will then have the pleasure of laying ourselves most humbly at our illustrious sovereign's feet, after a long absence. Meanwhile, I strive with the most sincere respect to be, and have the pleasure to remain for life, with the most humble submission

    In cantonment   Your Serene Highness
    At Point Levi   My most gracious Prince
    1 July 1783   And Lord's
                               Most humble servant,
                               Carl von Lindau

Letters to the Prince

Most Illustrious Hereditary Prince,
Gracious Sovereign and Lord!

Your Highness, I have the pleasure herewith, before our departure from Canada, most humbly to submit a report about Your Highness' Leib Company of the Hereditary Prince 1st Battalion, and to report those changes which have occurred since my last most humble report from the cantonment quarters at Point Levi, dated 1 July, such as that Musketeer Caspar Zeh deserted from our cantoment quarters at Point Levi on 13 July 1783, but returned to the company on the 20th of the same month. Corporals Bellinger and Tack, as well as 23 privates left the fortifications at Quebec on 13 July 1783, and returned to the company. The same occurred on 29 July, when four privates previously in Quebec on work detail, by the names of Nicholaus Schmidt, Daefner, Bruchausen, and Friedrich Hassler, returned. I must also most humbly report to Your Highness that the following six musketeers of the Leib Company were given their discharges on 21 July 1783, and departed: Jacob Flueckmann, Christoph Hessler, Theodor Kling, Henrich David, Jacob Schmidt, and Georg Deshmer. We were all embarked here on 1 August and supposedly are to set sail from here tomorrow. Meanwhile, until I have the pleasure to lay myself most humbly at Your Highness' feet, I strive with the most sincere respect to be

Letters to the Prince

On board the
Transport ship
Hero at Quebec
3 August 1783

Your Serene Highness
My most gracious Prince
And Lord's
Most humble servant,
von Lindau

- - - - - - -

Most Illustrious Hereditary Prince,
Gracious Sovereign and Lord!

Your Highness, I have the pleasure herewith to report our arrival at The Downs, on the tenth of this month, and most humbly to submit a report about Your Highness' Leib Company. I hope that Your Highness has already received the last report which I sent, dated 3 August on board the ship *Hero*, at Quebec. We arrived here safely on the tenth of this month after leaving Quebec 24 days ago, and I have the pleasure herewith most humbly to mention the changes which have occurred since my last report. I have met Sergeant Vaupel, Drummer Giese, and Private Remmy here. They were ordered to depart from Halifax to return to Your Highness' Company. Captain von Eschwege, as I have heard here, sailed for Stade with his troops five days prior to our arrival here. We are to sail from here with the first favorable wind. I long for the time when I can lay myself most humbly at Your Highness' feet, and personally assure Your Highness that throughout my life, I have the honor, with the greatest respect and submission, to be

Letters to the Prince

On board the
Transport ship
Hero, at The Downs,
Near Deal, England
16 September 1783

Your Serene Highness
My most gracious Prince
And Lord's
Most humble servant.
von Lindau

Most Illustrious Hereditary Prince,
Gracious Sovereign and Lord!

Your Highness, I have the pleasure herewith, most humbly, to send a report on Your Highness' Leib Company of the Hereditary Prince 1st Battalion, and to report that despite all precautions Drummer [Conrad] Seebach of the Leib Company deserted during the night of 30 September, in the previous month, from the small ship at Bremen. I exerted all my efforts to get him back, but failed to accomplish my purpose, because I later learned the Prussian recruiters had him. Your Highness can rest assured that I will not neglect to use all means and precautions to prevent further desertions.

I recommend myself to Your Highness' continued benevolence and favor, and strive with the most sincere respect to be

Rinteln
13 October 1783

Your Serene Highness
My most gracious Prince
And Lord's most humble
Servant,   v Lindau

Letters to the Prince

Most Illustrious Hereditary Prince,
Gracious Sovereign and Lord!

With the packet now departing, I have the pleasure, most humbly, to send a report about Your Highness' Leib Company of the 1st Battalion to Your Highness, and to mention that since my last most humbly submitted report, dated 13 October at Rinteln, the following changes have occurred. Musketeer Kuehn deserted on the thirteenth of the month, and Musketeers [Theophile] Schauer and Spanier, on the twenty-first of this month. With the first, Your Highness lost nothing, as he was completely worthless as a soldier, and he could have received his discharge from Colonel Lentz. I am especially sorry about the latter two, however, as they were two fine fellows. Colonel Lentz can vouch for me, to Your Highness, that this was not my fault. I also must report to Your Highness that Musketeer Herrmann was released with his discharge on the fourteenth of this month.

I wish and hope that Your Highness has received my previously submitted most humble reports. This is the seventh one that I have had the pleasure to send to Your Highness, since I have had the good fortune to command Your Highness' Company.

In the firm hope of Your Highness' most gracious satisfaction, I have the pleasure, with the most sincere submission and respect throughout my life, to be, and to remain

Letters to the Prince

On the Weser　　　　Your Serene Highness
Hannover Minden　　 My most gracious Prince
24 October 1783　　　And Lord's
　　　　　　　　　　Most humble servant,
　　　　　　　　　　Carl von Lindau
　　　　　　　- - - - - - -

Letters to the Prince

Most Illustrious Hereditary Prince,
Gracious Sovereign and Lord!

Your Highness has granted me the greatest pleasure and been pleased most graciously to promote me to staff captain by a directive of 20 July 1777. I received this on 7 October 1778, while in captivity at Winter Hill, near Boston. Your Highness, I give you the most humble and most meaningful thanks therefore, and from now on I will be even more diligent, and seek to make myself more worthy from day to day, so as to give my most gracious Prince the greatest pleasure and satisfaction.

I must also, most humbly, report to Your Highness that I was transferred on 8 October of the present year, as a 1st lieutenant from Your Highness' Leib Company in the regiment, and listed on the company report as a staff captain in Colonel von Gall's Company.

I recommend myself to Your Highness' greatest favor, and strive in complete submission to be

Winter Hill   Your Serene Highness'
15 October 1778   Most humble servant,
                              von Buttlar

Most Illustrious Hereditary Prince,
Gracious Sovereign and Lord!

Your Highness, I must most humbly report that on 29 April of the present year, Colonel von Gall, in the absence of Captain von Schoell, temporarily transferred command of Your Highness' Company to me. I will strive most diligently to administer this position so that I may enjoy Your Highness' most gracious satisfaction. Second Lieutenant von Eschwege has been promoted most graciously to 1st lieutenant, Ensign von Weyhers to 2nd lieutenant, and Cadet Burckhard to ensign. Ensign [Jacob] Heerwagen has been transferred as a 2nd lieutenant to Captain Schoell's Company, and Captain von Germann and Lieutenant Trott have been transferred from here to the Grenadier Company. Other than that, nothing has changed in the Leib Company. The men, in this critical situation, are all well and in good health.

Your Highness, I recommend myself to your continued favor and strive with the most sincere respect to be

Barracks at Your Serene Highness
Albemarle County My most gracious Prince's
in Virginia Most humble servant,
1 May 1780 von Buttlar

- - - - - - -

Letters to the Prince

Most Illustrious Hereditary Prince,
Gracious Sovereign and Lord!

May it please Your Highness to see in the accompanying report those occurrences within Your Highness' Company since the last report submitted by Captain von Germann.

It has been my responsibility, most gracious Prince, as I reported in my last most humble letter of 1 May 1780, since Colonel von Gall temporarily gave me supervision of the Leib Company, in place of Captain Schoell, to submit a report to Your Highness, when not prevented from doing so by other unavoidable circumstances. All letters sent out at this time must be sent, opened, to the Virginia governor. They are read by him, censored, and even returned so that no regimental reports can be forwarded.

Musketeer Grimm, who deserted on 4 April 1780, was made a prisoner of war again by an American patrol, and brought here. Musketeer Weingarten met a similar fate, having deserted on 21 June 1780 from these barracks, and been returned on 22 June. A few days earlier Musketeer [Philipp] Hinckel deserted, but despite all my efforts, I have not had the least information as to his fate, nor where he might be. The false assumption that a prisoner of war has a better chance of being exchanged than a Convention prisoner is the cause for these desertions, and it is difficult to convince young people, who are unaccustomed to misery, to have patience in this sad situation. Poor provisions and even a scarcity of food, together with high prices, are also contributing factors. Nevertheless, I spare no effort to console the men with the most convincing arguments, and the best hope is always to remember the illustrious and gracious father of our country, who constantly strives to provide for the welfare of his subjects.

The previously Cadet Burckhard has been promoted to ensign in Your Highness' Leib Company. The eagerness with which this young officer performs his duties leads me to hope for the best from him in the future, and I believe Your Highness can expect his continued excellent behavior.

If it were possible for me to be the motivation to cause every soldier to act properly and to perform well, like a prince, like the father of his country, like our Serene Highness, to serve such subjects with fairness, what good results my example and happy success would create in place of my lost satisfaction. Please forgive me, my most gracious Prince, for this comment, but I would be proud if I could make such a most humble report to Your Highness.

Musketeer Hallatschka, listed in the report as sick, has a bad abscess on his chest, which is no longer of a serious nature. Other than that, thank God, the men are all quite healthy.

I strive with the most sincere respect to be

Letters to the Prince

Barracks   Your Serene Highness
Albemarle County   My most gracious Prince's
4 July 1780   Most humble servant,
                        von Buttlar

- - - - - - -

Most Illustrious Hereditary Prince,
Gracious Sovereign and Lord!

May it please Your Highness to see all the changes and happenings in Your Highness' Leib Company, in the accompanying report of July last year, to which I now refer, and which was sent to Colonel von Gall at that time, has not yeet been forwarded, having met the same fate as all the other letters, and can only now, with this opportunity, be forwarded.

During this time, Musketeer Grimm returned again on 7 October from his desertion, but was noted in the report as a prisoner of war, because, after deserting from prison for prisoners of war at Winchester, he was again placed with Your Highness' regiment, and received permission from the commander of the local Provincials, upon his request, to remain with the regiment.

During this month of October, Drummer [Georg[Kitz deserted, and according to reports, which I received, set out at once for New York. Also, on the seventh of this month, a group of prisoners, including Weingarten, was sent away.

Letters to the Prince

In closing, I also note that I hope, Your Highness, in my next report, God willing, to be able to report that the Musketeer Hallatschka has fully recovered from the abcess on his chest. The rest of the men of the company, for now, thank God, are quite healthy.

Your Highness, I believe quite firmly, and patriotically wish, never again to be put in a position of being the instrument which must report events of this sort, which is required of me at all times, in my profession, as the most important of all my duties, to encourage to virtue and proper behavior, as it is within my power, the subjects of so gracious a father of his country, as Your Highness is.

    I strive with the most sincere respect, to be
Barracks in   Your Serene Highness
Albemarle County My most gracious Prince's
In Virginia   Most humble servant,
22 October 1780   von Buttlar

- - - - - - -

Most Illustrious Hereditary Prince,
    Gracious Sovereign and Lord!

May it please Your Highness to see in the accompanying report the changes in Your Highness' Leib Company.

Drummer Kitz returned again from his

desertion on 19 November. On orders of Colonel von Gall, Musketeers Schweinsberger and Fuhr are leaving the company on details. The first has been recalled to Hanau by Your Highness' orders, and the latter has been transferred to the Hesse-Hanau Jaeger Corps in Canada. I have the pleasure, most humbly, to refer to my next to last report of 22 October of last year. The rest of the company, thank God, is in good health. Musketeer Hallatschka is improving from day to day, and all of us, most humble servants, wish nothing more than after such a long time, soon to enjoy the good fortune of being able to fall at our most Illustrious Prince's feet.

We have the misfortune now of being escorted from here to the province of Maryland. Excuse me, illustrious Prince, for my melancholy, always to be at a distance from our truest provider and father of our country, in a world, where we are at opposite poles from our fatherland, to sigh in an eternal captivity, where, tearfully, we constantly remember our illustrious and gracious Prince.

Your Highness, be so kind as to permit me to ask a most humble favor for Musketeer Wiskemann. It concerns his enlistment, which has already exceeded his commitment by nearly three years. He came in while I was writing this letter, and asked as he had already served three years

Letters to the Prince

beyond his enlistment, if he could reenlist for a new six year period. I submit myself on this point completely to what it may please Your Highness to order.

As our worthy colonel leaves us tomorrow, having been exchanged, we also wish to be able to follow him soon, and this loss, as much as it causes us pain, gives us the hope that he will intercede for us.

I strive with the most sincere respect, to be

Barracks in Your Serene Highness
Albemarle County My most gracious Prince's
In Virginia Most humble servant,
29 November 1780 von Buttlar

- - - - - - - -

Most Illustrious Hereditary Prince,
Gracious Sovereign and Lord!

May it please Your Highness most graciously to see in the accompanying report what changes have occurred since the departure of Colonel von Gall, who took my last report to Your Highness on 29 August 1780 to New York with him, until the present, in Your Highness' Leib Company. In my next to last report, I mentioned that we had received marching orders to march from this province of Virginia, to the province of Maryland, in order to be held there. The English troops, at that time, had already marched, but because they could only be accommodated in this province with great difficulty, it was decided that the German troops would not leave Virginia this winter, and so far it has not happened.

A short time ago however, an event occurred whereby an English fleet entered the harbor at Richmond, a port about ninety English miles from here, and as the troops, which were on board had landed, we received the hasty order, at that time, to march. The baggage and sick individuals were left behind, and we were taken thirty miles from here, where we had to bivouac in the woods, until after the English again had departed from Richmond. County. We then received the order to march back to the Barracks in Albemarle County

During this opportunity, Musketeer Baecker deserted from Your Highness' Company. Previously, he had had leave to work in the country in order to earn something, and after receiving the order to return to the company, he remained away. However, I am certainly convinced that he has not been lost, but will submit a letter requesting pardon to the regiment.

Musketeer Hallerschka is worse each day from his bad abscess, and I greatly fear that it will become completely disabling.

Musketeer Weingarten, who was among the prisoners of war, fortunately was exchanged with

Letters to the Prince

the artillerymen captured at Bennington, and is currently in New York according to reliable information.

The rest of the men of the company, thank God, are all still healthy.

I strive with the most sincere respect, to be

Barracks in
Albemarle County
in Virginia
29 January 1781

Your Serene Highness
My most gracious Prince's
Most humble servant,
von Buttlar

Most Illustrious Prince,
Gracious Sovereign and Lord!

May it please Your Highness most graciously to see what has occurred in Your Highness' Leib Company since Lieutenant von Eschwege submitted the most humble report, during the time when I had to remain behind sick, at the Barracks in Albemarle County, in Virginia.

Upon my arrival at the regiment in Winchester, the officers of the Convention troops had already been separated from the soldiers. The German regiments marched into the barracks, and the officers received orders to take quarters within a radius of about seven or eight miles of Winchester, with the special restriction that no one was to go to his regiment, nor to have any connection with the soldiers.

Letters to the Prince

After we had been in this arrangement for seven weeks, both officers and men received orders; the first to go to Windsor in the province of Connecticut, the latter to march to Reading in Pennsylvania. The regiment moved out one day ahead of the officers, and the officers were given a special march route. We met our regiment again at Reading in Pennsylvania, about 45 miles from Philadelphia, but were allowed to remain in the city for only one night. We had to obtain information about the company surreptitiously, and I have the pleasure Your Highness, to submit my most humble report.

According to information which Lieutenant Colonel Lentz provided for us, Ensign Burckhard, on Your Highness' orders, had his rank taken away, and is listed in the report under the number of privates, as a cadet. Musketeer Kohlep returned from his desertion, and Hautboist Insdorf, Sr., and Musketeer Hallatschka have recovered. Both Hautboists Mueller and Insdorf, Jr., granted eight days of leave by Lieutenant Colonel Lentz, before the march out of Allbemarle County in Virginia, have returned on time. Musketeers Wiskemann, and Auffleider, Hueffner, [Johannes] Seltzer, and Drummer Kitz have deserted since we were separated from them. Both Musketeers Krieg and Kempf, who were ordered to remain behind with the baggage, when we marched out of Albemarle County, have once again returned to the company. Musketeer [Johann Adam] Bohlaender married near Lancaster in Pennsylvania, after requesting permission to marry, from Lieutenant Colonel Lentz and me, and who might have deserted if refused. However, his marriage lasted only three weeks, and, as his wife has died, I did not consider it necessary to make my most humble report about it.

As difficult as it may be to get news about the regiment in the future, I will still try with my best effort and most conscientious attention to duty, most humbly to submit the most recent and most exact reports to Your Highness.

I have the honor, with the most sincere respect, to be

East Windsor
in the province
of Connecticut
23 August 1781

Your Serene Highness'
Most humble servant,
von Buttlar

- - - - - - -

Letters to the Prince

Most Illustrious Hereditary Prince,
Gracious Sovereign and Lord!

Your Highness, I must most humbly report that to our absolute greatest joy, on the past 13 September, at East Windsor, in the province of Connecticut, all the Convention officers of Burgoyne's army received our exchange. However, we did not leave East Windsor until 5 October and arrived on the eleventh, happily, in New York.

I hope and wish from the bottom of my heart, that Your Highness has received my last company report of 28 August, in which I made the most accurate report since our separation from our men, and about their last situation, as we noted at Reading in Pennsylvania, as we marched through. Since then, despite every effort, I have not been able to obtain the least additional information.

I brought two drummers, two lance corporals, and three privates with me here to New York, who were all brought along under the designation of officers' servants. These were Drummers [Jacob] Gewald and Giese, Lance Corporals [Philipp] Heintzinger and Krieg, and Privates Hallatschka, Bohlaender, and [Friedrich] Kaiser. All of us are presently in New York, but during the coming days are to go to Long Island, where we are to remain until the coming spring, when we are to be sent to Canada.

Second Lieutenant Weyhers is to go with the

Letters to the Prince

English fleet from here to Virginia, in order to serve with the Hesse [Cassel] Grenadiers, because they have many sick officers at this time, and he drew the short straw. Five officers from our regiment are going along on this expedition, and two from the Duke of Brunswick's troops. For my part, I would have gladly gone, but the Hessian Lieutenant General von Knyphausen only wanted fifteen subaltern officers.

I recommend myself to Your Highness' continued favor, and strive with the most sincere respect, to be

New York Your Serene Highness
15 October 1781 My most gracious Prince's
Most humble servant,
von Buttlar

- - - - - - -

Most Illustrious Prince,
Gracious Sovereign and Lord!

Your Highness, I must most humbly report that Cadet Burckhard has been recalled to Hanau on Your Highness' most gracious order. The two musketeers, Heintzinger and Hallatschka are going with him, having been sent by Lieutenant Colonel Lentz. Finally, the lieutenant colonel wished to send Musketeer Krieg of Your Highness' Leib Company with them. However, I made a suggestion to him that the above mentioned Musketeer Hallatschka should be sent, because the abscess on his neck has worsened again, and he has completely lost his voice. As a

Letters to the Prince

result, he no longer can be used on field service. The colonel agreed with me at once, and made it known in orders.

First Lieutenant von Eschwege is presently on a detail at Denyce's Ferry, not far from Staten Island, and from Your Highness' Leib Company of the 1st Battalion, he has Drummer Giese and Privates Krieg, Bohlaender, and Kaiser with him.

Second Lieutenant von Weyhers has not yet returned with the fleet, which sailed from New York to Virginia.

Finally, I recommend myself to Your Highness' continued favor and strive with the most sincere respect, to be

Flushing on	Your Serene Highness
Long Island	My most gracious Prince's
Near New York	Most humble servant,
5 November 1781	von Buttlar

- - - - - - - -

Most Illustrious Hereditary Prince,
Gracious Sovereign and Lord!

It pleased Your Highness to order Lieutenant Colonel von Janecke to leave 200 weapons behind at Muenden for the 1st Battalion, which order he found here upon his arrival.

In accordance with Your Highness' order, Lieutenant Colonel Janecke told me I could receive these 200 weapons on Monday, 13 October, but I would be required to give him a receipt, that I had received the weapons in the best condition. However, because the weapons were in an especially poor condition and rusted, in short, in a condition that they could not be repaired in less than fourteen days, and at a great cost, I refused to accept the weapons in exchange for the requested receipt. I agreed with Adjutant [Nicolaus] Schweinebraten to leave the weapons, protected in cases, in the house of the merchant Eckhardt, until the arrival of Colonel Lentz. If he would accept them, then the merchant Eckhardt would be given a receipt that 200 weapons had been taken from the cases. I thought, most illustrious Hereditary Prince, that this was a situation - as the captain of the Free Corps would not deliver good weapons, it was all that I could do.

Day before yesterday, being 16 October, I sent to the merchant Eckhardt's house to ask if the weapons were in a place where they would not be further ruined, and received to my surprise, the information in writing, that after the agreement made between Adjutant Schweinebraten and me, at the merchant Eckhardt's house, the adjutant had delivered another order, namely to deliver the weapons and all the other arms to Hanau - and they were gone. As my proof, I can produce this letter. I must not neglect, most humbly, to report this incident to Your Highness, and leave it most humbly to Your Highness' discretion to

Letters to the Prince

dispose of as you please.

I was here on 12 October, and now wait impatiently on the battalion. First, it is said they can be here in six days, then in ten days. As soon as I have confirmed reports as to where the battalion is, I will not fail to sail a day's trip toward it, in order to obtain my orders. Ansbach troops have been here since yesterday, waiting for a transport. The Weser is surprisingly low. Because of this situation, the troops often travel barely two and one-half miles per day.

I strive with the most sincere submission, to be

Muenden   Your Serene Highness
18 October 1783   My most gracious Prince's
                        Most humble servant,
                           von Buttlar

- - - - - - -

Letters to the Prince

Most Illustrious Landgrave,
Gracious Hereditary Prince and Lord!

May it please Your Highness to allow me to present the circumstances which put me in the necessity, most humbly, to seek a gracious release from the war service, from Your Highness. Your Highness most graciously knows, without my saying it, that I am completely alone, and as a result had to transfer my property to strangers when I marched away. I also have six younger sisters, who as they are still somewhat dependent upon me, tie me to them.

Except for this, and the all too great distance from Your Highness, I would consider it my greatest good fortune to spend the rest of the days of my life in Your Highness' service.

I seek with longing the most gracious consent to my most humble request, and strive with the most humble respect, to be

    From the camp   Illustrious Landgrave
    At Castleton   Most gracious Hereditary
    19 July 1777   Prince and Lord
                          Your Serene Highness'
                          Most humble and truly
                          obedient servant,
                          Friedrich von Schachten

- - - - - - -

Letters to the Prince

Sir,

In accordance with orders, you have here in writing my release from the military service of His Serene Highness. The care of my estate, which I have had to entrust to strangers, as I, as is known, am alone, could result in great damage to me because of the length of time and the great distance, as well as a considerable loan, which I, as eldest family member, received from the Electoral petit court, which, as is known, can be charged to me personally, and which final indulgence ends during the present year. All these are the reasons which make it absolutely necessary, even though I had wished to spend my entire lifetime in the service of my most gracious master.

His Highness will, such being the case, as a result of my most humble request, graciously consent to release me after the end of this campaign.

In camp near   von Schachten
Castleton
14 July 1777

- - - - -

Most Illustrious Landgrave,
Gracious Hereditary Prince and Lord!

May Your Highness most graciously allow my most humble request to Your Highness, submitted two years ago, through Colonel von Gall, concerning my release from military service, to be repeated here.

Letters to the Prince

Your Highness is already aware, without my saying so, that I still have six sisters, all of whom are primarily dependent upon me, and that furthermore, all my property had to be transferred to strangers, when I marched away, which can only result in great damage to me because of the length of time, and the distance involved.

How happy I would be if I could finish my days in the service of the most gracious Prince without worrying about such circumstances.

I flatter myself, Your Highness will honor my most humble request because of the reasons given. Therefore, I venture to unite that request with another most humble request, to be provided most graciously with free transportation to Germany.

I strive in the most sincere humbleness to be

At the barracks   Most Illustrious Landgrave
Near   Gracious Hereditary Prince
Charlottesville   and Lord
25 September 1779   Your Serene Highness'
                  Most humble and truly
                  obedient servant,
                  Fr. Von Schachten

- - - - - - -

Most Illustrious Landgrave,
Gracious Sovereign of the Land,
And Lord

Your Highness, herewith I lay myself, most

humbly, at Your Highness' feet, to present the following problem. Since we have been in this country, we have been in the brigade of Major General Phillips, the chief and commander of the English Artillery. How unpleasant it is for us to have a chief to whom one can not speak nor explain things, and who does not even have an adjutant who can speak to him [for us]. All orders, which we receive from him, are written, part in French, part in English, and we must guess or run around for a long time, until we find someone who will be kind enough to clarify them. How dangerous that is for us, and how easily our honor could be lost, by the failure to understand such an order. We approach our duty with the greatest timidity which can be imagined. All our thoughts turn to receiving an actual satisfaction from the illustrious father of our country, as long as we are able, most humbly, to serve Your Highness. The duty which we are required to perform with the English Artillery, since our assignment, is that we are forced by our chief, according to their system, to learn a new drill, with the understanding that in all things we will be held to the same standard, according to the promise of Major General Phillips, and considering the service, that appears to be the situation. However, we have the greatest reason to complain to Your Highness about the pay for the battalion equipment and forage money, as the most junior English artillery lieutenant received

Letters to the Prince

72 pounds sterling during the past year. Even an overseer who has a grade comparable to our servant supervisor, receives 25 pounds sterling. On the other hand, while we have performed the identical service from the beginning, and during the late campaign, did not serve an hour with our German troops. Even during that time, we were paid only 12 pounds, 17 shillings. When I asked our chief, General Phillips why, in this case we were not considered on an equal footing with his officers, and I told him we had reason to complain about that, he tried to make all sorts of excuses. Although I tried my best to make him understand that that gave us a reason to be dissatisfied, when he could find no other excuse, he said the money which had been paid to his artillery officers was an extraordinary allowance from His Royal Majesty. As the [treaty] articles were known by me, I pointed out the article in which it is stated that all allowances, which it pleased His Majesty to grant, such as in this case, where we had to serve with them, were to be paid to the [German] troops in the same proportion. Although I mentioned this in all the arguments, nevertheless, we have received nothing more. I can come to no other conclusion than that he means do us wrong.

We live in hope that Your Highness will be so kind as to assist us in this so great loss, especially since we have had to move into expensive winter quarters, which cost us two-thirds more than the officers of all the other German troops, and which everyone can attest he is forced to go into debt against his wishes, which would not be the case, if we were paid the allowance money in the same proportion as the English Artillery.

Several days ago, another list was submitted in order to receive 200 days' of the bonus money, and again it is to be paid out as in the past years.

This is once more a new reason for us to lay ourselves at Your Highness' feet, and most humbly to ask Your Highness to take note of our present condition, and to make such changes as possible, or if it pleases to do the favor, after this coming, and finally ended campaign, in case there is improvement to be hoped for, with the greatest kindness, to remove me from continued service, for His [Britannic] Majesty in America.

In the most humbler assurance of receiving one or the other most gracious requests, I lay myself in most sincere submission at Your Highness' feet.

From the   Your Serene Highness'
winter quarters Most humble servant,
1 May 1777   [Wilhelm] Dufais

- - - - - - -

Most Illustrious Hereditary Prince,
Gracious Sovereign and Lord!

Your Highness, the latest news received

concerning my family and the economic condition of my household, compels me most humble to present my case to Your Highness, and to ask for my most humble release from my service. My personal presence is urgently needed in order not to suffer irreparable damage for the rest of my life. And to this is added, that our kind is not the best here, and so constituted that it can be distinguished from one of the most fatiguing wars in Germany only by the most far-reaching comparison of its necessary baggage transport, which is at risk daily if allowed to remain in place. As a result, one is robbed of everything necessary to maintain his health.

Second - Because of the high prices in this land, it is necessary to add money [to the pay received].

Third - Because we officers of the German Artillery are not considered equal to the [Royal] Artillery, as to the allowances for battalion baggage and forage, as a lieutenant receives 72 pounds sterling, and, I and the others, only 12 pounds, 17 Shillings, and some received that for a full year, and we will not receive more in the future, although we must perform the same and equal duties with one another.

Finally, it is said that because of the previous year's affair on Lake Champlain, the English Artillery officers were to have been paid another unannounced special allowance, about which my captain and I can learn little, and have not received the least amount.

Letters to the Prince

These stated, weighty reasons, especially however, the first letter, which I and the others most humbly laid at Your Highness' feet, gives me the most assured hope for a gracious consent to my most humble request, for which, all my life and unceasingly, remain in most sincere submission

In camp at   Your Serene Highness'
East Creek   Most humble,
12 July 1777   Dufais

- - - - - - -

Most Humble Memorial

After seeing in the most recently received letter from Hanau, that my family and household economic conditions, which, in order not to suffer an irreparable loss for the rest of my life, demand my personal presence most urgently.

Second - Because of the high prices in this land, it is necessary to add money [to the pay received].

Third - We officers of the German Artillery are not considered equal to the royal [Artillery] as to the allowances for battalion baggage and forage, as each lieutenant receives 72 pounds sterling, and I, and the other officers only, 12 pounds, 17 schillings, and some pence, per year, and are to receive no more in the future, although we must perform the same and equal duties with one another.

Finally, it is said that because of the previous year's affair on Lake Champlain, the English officers

Letters to the Prince

were to have been paid another unannounced special allowance about which my captain and I can learn little, and have not received the least amount.

These stated weighty reasons, especially however, the first letter, causes me finally, most humbly, to request my discharge. May you sir, therefore, do me the favor of requesting my release from His Highness. With this hope, I have the honor, with the most sincere respect, to remain

        Sir,
        Your most humble servant,
        Dufais

Letters to the Prince

Most Illustrious Hereditary Prince,
Gracious Sovereign and Lord!

As I have been so unfortunate as to earn Your Highness' disfavor, which was reported to me by my brother in two of his letters, I throw myself at Your Highness' feet and ask forgiveness for my failure, which occurred in the following manner, and for which I had not the least fault. When we had the misfortune several years ago to end up in captivity, it was at the same time my great misfortune to be very sick, and so miserable that I could no longer stand. Therefore, I saw it as necessary during the march through the wilderness to remain behind, but as soon as my strength allowed, I intended to join the regiment in which I had always conducted myself as a proper soldier, and will always do this as long as I have the pleasure to be in Your Highness' service.

I confess that nothing has grieved me more than this, as my future fate hangs in Your Highness' hands, and if I lose that, all my prospects for the future of my life are destroyed.

Gracious Prince and Lord, again grant me your favor, which I had before, and allow me to be as fortunate as I can be. If I had not committed the error, I would demonstrate through irreproachable conduct, that you do not waste your favor on an unappreciative individual.

I lay myself most humbly at Your Highness' feet,

and strive to the end of my life, with true diligence and most sincere submission, to be

  Quebec   Your Serene Highness
  25 October 1781 My most gracious Sovereign
          And Lord's
         Most humble servant,
         Friedrich Wilhelm von Pape

- - - - - - -

  Most Illustrious Landgrave and Hereditary Prince,
    Gracious Sovereign and Lord!

Your Highness, I have the great pleasure by this means, most humbly, to report that we received the last ship's provisions on the transport ship *Free Briton* on 12 October at Cuxhaven. On the thirteenth, at two-thirty we were landed, and at four o'clock we marched out of Ritzebuettel, and at ten o'clock in the evening arrived at quarters in Dorum, in Hannover, having been escorted there by Lieutenant von Succow. The following men deserted during the night: 1) Grenadier Schlegel 2) Grenadier Schneider, II 3) Grenadier Fritz, and 4) Grenadier Binmueller.

At six o'clock on the morning of the fourteenth, general march was beaten, at six-thirty assembly, and at seven o'clock march, whereupon we at once moved out and marched to Bremerlehe, where we embarked on four small Weser ships. Tattoo was beaten at eight-thirty in the evening. Reveille was at six o'clock on the morning of the fifteenth, and we left the ships at nine o'clock in order to be mustered, passing before a Hannover Dragoon Major Niemayer. At twelve o'clock, tonight we are to sail from here toward Bremen.

In the absence of other orders, I have paid all the men according to the roster, as Captain Schunck has paid them on the march on land.

I have had to keep Captain Wiederhold, because of his behavior and his continued drunkenness, even while under arrest, in arrest to this time, as I have received no resolution to my first most humble report.

I wish nothing more than that all actions, which I and Lieutenant Steller do with all our efforts, according to what we presume to be Your Highness' gracious intent, really satisfy Your Highness, and that I might console myself with Your Highness' greatest satisfaction.

As soon as I have the opportunity to send off letters, I will quickly do so, and now and throughout my lifetime, be with the most sincere respect

[n.p., n.d.]   Most Illustrious Landgrave and
                    Hereditary Prince
                    Gracious Sovereign and Lord
                    Your Serene Highness'
                    Most humble and truly
                    Obedient servant,
                    Zincke,   Lieutenant

Letters to the Prince

Most Illustrious Hereditary Prince,
Gracious Sovereign and Lord!

I have already had the greatest pleasure to serve as adjutant in Your Highness' 1st Battalion - without bragging, with the greatest exactness and satisfaction of my superior staff officers. In the beginning, for more than one and one-half years, I did not enjoy the least advantage from this position, except my second lieutenant pay at that time, according to the Hesse-Hanau pay scale, although I often made various representations about it to our then commander, Colonel von Gall, that not only were my activities incomparably greater than any other subaltern, but also that my position and expenses connected therewith, to this duty, could not be fulfilled on a second lieutenant's pay. Not withstanding, he always consoled me with reference to the Duke of Brunswick's pay scale, with the added comment that if that scale were most graciously implemented by Your Highness, I would also receive the same pay, that a Duke of Brunswick's adjutant actually has. With that hope, I flattered myself until 1 October 1777, when by an order from the then Colonel von Gall, the Brunswick pay scale was introduced in the 1st Battalion. And since that time, I have been given the same pay as the Duke of Brunswick's adjutant. However, in a gracious directive, dated 19 April 1781, effective on 6 March 1782, I see to my serious disadvantage, that the adjutant and regimental quartermaster are to have their pay significantly reduced from now on. Therefore, I submit my most humble request to Your Highness, to do me the favor, that if in the future, according to Your Highness' most gracious order, I am to continue performing the duty as adjutant, that my pay also be made according to the pay scale of the Duke of Brunswick's adjutant. However, if this does not please Your Highness, I would consider myself most fortunate, if it would please Your Highness, graciously, to release me completely from the adjutant duty, and that once again, I might perform duty in the company, simply as a second lieutenant, because I am unable, without disadvantage to myself, to defray the expenses incurred by the adjutant position, on only the pay of a second lieutenant. I lay myself, therefore, most humbly, at Your Highness' feet, and seek a most gracious resolution to my humble request, and as my constant goal will be to make myself even more worthy of Your Highness' favor, my future striving will always be, and I will never cease to be, with the most sincerely respectful submission

Bedford on Your Serene Highness'
Long Island Most humble servant,
17 March 1782 Heerwagen

- - - - - - -

Letters to the Prince

Most Illustrious Hereditary Prince,
Gracious Sovereign and Lord!

Your Highness, allow most graciously that I herewith presume, most humbly, to ask Your Highness to grant the greatest favor, of those favors so abundantly conferred upon me by Your Highness, during the many years of military service, which I have had the pleasure to spend in Your Highness' military, and, graciously, authorize my release. Also, although I am convinced of Your Highness' most gracious and well-meaning intentions, I fear that Your Highness might refuse my most humble request, because my complete happiness is solely dependent thereon. I lay myself in most humble appreciation at your feet, with the warmest feelings of respect for the greatest favor with which Your Highness ever could honor me.

I have the pleasure to hope for the most gracious granting of this, my last most humble request, and strive with the most sincere humbleness to be

In camp at   Your Serene Highness
Point Levi   My most gracious Hereditary
19 October 1783   Prince and Lord's
                      Most humble and truly
                      Obedient servant, Lieutenant
                      Friedrich Ludwig Kempffer

Letters to the Prince

Most Illustrious Hereditary Prince,
Gracious Sovereign and Lord!

All the officers of the Hesses-Hanau Infantry Regiment Hereditary Prince, knowing that Ensign Burckhard, in a gracious directive of 2 November 1780, had not only his rank, but also his pay rescinded thereby, all attest that this Burckhard has demonstrated a good character, and greatly regret his sad fate, and most humbly beg Your Highness to pardon this unfortunate individual.

We remain with the most sincere respect
Your Serene Highness'
Most humble servants,
Scheel, von Germann, von Buttlar
Von Geyling, von Trott, von Eschwege,
Bischhausen, von Richtersleben,
Von Weyhers, Heerwagen, Weitzel
Dufais, Bacumerth, Sartorius

- - - - - - -

Letters to the Prince

Most Illustrious Landgrave and Hereditary Prince, Gracious Sovereign and Lord!

Your Highness, forgive the most humble lines of an unhappy individual, whose tears dare to approach Your Highness' throne. The sorry fate in which I find myself, most illustrious Prince, and the pain which crushes me to the ground, stifles the feeling in my heart, whose blood in the innermost recesses pounds for the greatness of his Prince. Forgive my Illustrious Hereditary Prince, for an inspiration whose basis is despair and whose support is innocence.

The fate which created my happiness, cast me down in misfortune, the more terrible to feel. Indeed, an entire world full of misery confronted me, whose bitterness the philosophical strength of each moral must stifle. A gracious commission for an ensign's position was given to me on 1 May 1780 by Colonel and Commander von Gall, with an order to Lieutenant and Regimental Quartermaster Sartorius that I was to receive 100 pounds sterling.

Pressed by the most vigorous appreciation, without giving thought to the shadow of doubt of my present unfortunate situation, I hastened in my innocence to express my appreciation to my illustrious Prince in a most humble letter that day. The honor of my colonel awoke sufficient confidence in me, supposing, without the least suspicion, the validity of the most gracious commission, and may God be the avenger of my guilt in the knowledge of a deed which could make me so unhappy.

I implore, I entreat, I weep at Your Highness' feet, most gracious Prince. Do not let me be the victim because my crime is innocence. Like the ocean which encircles the inhabited earth, Your Highness' comforting soul embraces every class, every age of mankind. Yes, great Prince, you welcome those who come to your humane altars. Embrace this pure innocence of an unfortunate who has nothing comparable with the incense of flattery. The innocence is intrepid enough (please excuse this expression, illustrious Prince), dressed in innocence, to approach a throne, and how delightful it is to have one such guarantee of happiness, such as mine, whose country rests on pillars supported by innocence and justice.

All the officers of Your Highness' regiment, if my word is insufficient, are ready voluntarily to bear witness to my claim of being a worthy officer (during the time when I was convinced of the propriety of my commission), as I have always striven, as an individual, to fulfill the wishes of Lieutenant Colonel Lentz, my present commander, who is in Your Highness' Regiment. My bleeding heart, gracious Prince, does not ease my pain, and if I were not inwardly convinced of Your Highness' charity, my grief would degenerate into complete despair, because

Letters to the Prince

I still maintain my innocence.

    I strive respectfully in the pursuit of my humble request, and remain in constant respect

    Lancaster   Your Serene Highness
    7 July 1781   Most humble, obedient servant,
                    Ludwig Theodor Burckhard

    Most Illustrious Prince,
    Gracious Sovereign and Lord!

On Your Highness' order, I am returning now from America, after sailing on board the ship *Amazon*, on 15 December of the past year from New York, with Lieutenant Thoma, Sergeant Majors Staff and [Christoph] Dehnhard, and Musketeers Heintzinger and Hallatschka, both of Your Highness' Leib Company, and arriving safely on 14 January of this year at Portsmouth, with the four invalids mentioned above. The positive order of Lieutenant Lentz to continue my march as soon as I had taken care of the necessities for the invalids, and the package which had to be delivered quickly, and which I was to have the great pleasure of most humbly delivering to Your Highness, made it necessary for me, also, after I had taken care of the mentioned invalids, as well as my abilities allowed, to go from Portsmouth to London, and to ask what should be done with the invalids who returned from America. On 15 January, we learned that a ship had arrived from Canada, with men of Your

Highness' troops on board. On this ship were: Lieutenant [Friedrich] Jung of Your Highness' Jaeger Corps, and Captain-at-arms Kirchkoff, and Musketeers Kolep, [Christoph] Diehl, [Philipp] Ruehl, [Conrad] Bickes, and Wetter, of Your Highness' 1st Battalion. These men had the misfortune that the ship *Dispatch*, on which they had embarked at Quebec, foundered at Baltimore in Ireland, and the mast crushed Musketeer [Philipp Jacob] Heyl to death. Thereafter, they were embarked on another ship named *Little Deal*, and sailed from there to Portsmouth. Now, Lieutenant Thoma will have the great pleasure of providing more exact information about these men to Your Highness.

We arrived in London on the evening of 19 January, and visited all the applicable institutions for the men who had been left behind in Portsmouth. We went to Major [Carl August] Kitzleben, who promised us most sincerely to care for Your Highness' troops, that they would be taken with the Hesse-[Cassel] invalids, as soon as those individuals arrived in Portsmouth, to Chatham, a royal hospital in London, and they would have to wait for the ship, which was bringing recruits, heading to America from Germany, and they would then go back to Germany with the same ship. We gave him a list of our men, and gave them our best recommendation, and did the same to Captain Bailey of the 62nd Regiment, and to the merchant von Notten. I also have the great pleasure, Your Highness, to send herewith my complete experiences in London, and then we will go, by the earliest opportunity, to Margate, and from there to Ostend, and thus I will have the great pleasure, the soonest, to throw myself at Your Highness' feet.

The sadness which constantly depresses me, disappears the closer I approach to Your Highness' throne, and my fate is clearly the best, as it is in Your Highness' worthy hands.

I strive with the most sincere respect, to be
London   Your Serene Highness'
24 January 1782   Most humble servant,
                    Ludwig Theodor Burckhard

- - - - - - -

Portsmouth, [on board the] ship *Little Deal*
13 January 1782
Honorable Sir, High and Mighty Colonel

On orders of Captain von Schoell, whose packet to you is attached most humbly, the listed troops are with me as lance corporals: Ewald, Kohlep, Diehl, Ruehl, Bickes, Wetter, and Heyl. Also, one invalid, by the name of Jacob Mueller, has been ordered to embark with us on the fleet sailing for Germany. We were embarked on the ship *Fare* on 19 October of last year, then transferred to the ship *Little Deal* after a few days, but the day before sailing, we were embarked on the ship *Dispatch*. At that time, Lieutenant Jung of the Hesse-Hanau Jaegers was assigned with us. We sailed on 16 November of last year from the Island of Pic [Bic], in Canada, and after tolerating many miseries and daily storms, we arrived on 12 December at Baltimore in Ireland, after the entire fleet had been scattered. Here we remained at anchor from 12 to 27 December, because during the night, in the harbor, we experienced the most frightful storm. Both anchors broke loose, our ship ran aground on the rocks, and we all saved only our lives from the greatest threat of death, during the very dark night. The mainmast which stuck out of the earth, crushed Philipp Jacob Heyl's skull and leg, and he died within a few minutes, and was thrown into the water by the waves, which caused the ship to roll back and forth, severely. Musketeer Bickes was seriously injured, Diehl and Kohlep injured on the head; Ruehl hurt on the arm, while I, in the greatest danger of losing my life, at four o'clock at night, when all the people were already on land, thought of nothing but to same my lord's dispatches.

The thieving inhabitants of Ireland tried to rob us of everything, even the things held in our hands. I lay myself down with my chest on the dispatches, in order to save them, and thank God, I was able to keep them. Even the 11 guineas, 15 shillings, which had been given to me for the men, was taken from me in a thieving manner by the inhabitants. I recognized the

Letters to the Prince

man who had my money in his hand, but more than 300 residents, claiming the right of salvage, wounded me and Musketeer Wetter, and we thank God that we could save our lives. Along the most wretched road, we then went 47 miles on foot to Cove, to rejoin the fleet and were embarked on this ship.

We were told we would sail to London in eight days, but how we will continue onward, we still do not know. Tomorrow a doctor is coming from Portsmouth to tend to my injuries. Furthermore, I must most humbly report that the invalid Mueller died on 24 October on board the ship, and I had him buried on land the next day.

This packet, which I have brought with me, was ordered by Captain von Schoell to be forwarded immediately upon our arrival in England, because I can not know how long we are to remain in England.

     Your most humble servant,
     Captain-at-arms Kirchoff

Letters to the Prince

Most Illustrious Hereditary Prince,
Gracious Sovereign and Lord!

May it please Your Highness, graciously to accept the enclosed journal of the expedition to Charleston, and the accompanying map. [Missing] As I had the opportunity to copy it for Captain Gerlach, quartermaster general on General von Riedesel's staff, who is here, and as it may not have reached Your Highness' hand in such a complete form, I considered it my most humble duty, with the permission of said captain, to lay it most submissively at Your Highness' feet, and to ask Your Highness' most gracious favor and most devoted remembrance.

I strive in most sincere submissiveness, to be
Your Serene Highness'
Truly most humble servant and subject,
Andreas Koch
Quartermaster Sergeant of Lieutenant
Colonel Lentz' Company

- - - - - - -

Most Illustrious Landgrave
and Hereditary Prince,
Gracious Sovereign and Lord!

Your Highness will already most graciously know

Letters to the Prince

from the reports submitted that I was severely wounded during the affair at Bennington on the 16th of August of last year. I originally hoped that my wound would be of a nature which would not prevent my remaining in Your Highness' service in the future, so that I could make myself more fortunate and more worthy of Your Highness' special favor. Unfortunately, due to the poorly organized English open field hospital, with the negligent care by the English doctors therein, whose services I had to have initially, and which were of the most intermittent sort, I often went three days without being bandaged, and added thereto was the miserable retreat for the wounded, and finally, as a result of the entire army being captured, the lack of transportation made it necessary, as I could not remain in the hospital, to follow the company. I was always in hope, however, that I would have a quick recovery and quickly be able to resume my duty, but my wound grew so much worse from these fatal conditions, despite our Regimental Surgeon Heidelbach having done everything possible, and providing excellent care, while I was under his care, and which I definitely desired, I now no longer have more than a hope of recovery of this shattered member, and throughout my life will have a lame and useless right arm, to which Regimental Surgeon Heidelbach also attests to Your Highness, with the proof, which he will present to Your Highness. These, gracious Sovereign and Lord, are the reasons which cause me to throw myself at Your Highness' most gracious feet, and unfortunately I see it as necessary, most humbly, to request my recall to Germany. Although, at the same time, I am convinced and assured of Your Hightness' gracious benevolence and praise, especially that Your Highness would always be pleased to have an excellent and gracious goal for an officer who had striven with diligence and loyalty to perform duty for his most gracious Prince, therefore, I make for myself the already beforehand pleasant assurance that I have Your Highness' greatest pleasure to enjoy in these perplexing unfortunate situations, so that I and my family can be further maintained, supported, and educated.

In this most confident hope of Your Highness' most gracious favor, I strive with the most unbounded respectful humiliation, to be
    Your Serene Highness' most humble servant,
      Carl Dittmar Spangenberg, Lieutenant

Letters to the Prince

That Lieutenant Carl Dittmar Spangenberg, of His Serene Highness and Hereditary Prince of Hesse-Cassel's illustrious Artillery Corps, was wounded by a small ball in the affair at Bennington, on 16 August of last year. The ball entered at the lower angle of the shoulder blade, splitting, during its passage, not only the joint of the shoulder bones, but also the upper arm bone, near the end of the joint, which was cut out by a surgeon, and he then lay seven weeks under the care and dressing of an English doctor in the flying camp hospital. Then, due to disturbances and poor transportation, the damaged bones developed an infection from a lack of proper care, and thus made the healing more difficult until now, despite the best care by me. Now, however, there appears hope of healing, after which the mentioned lieutenant will remain lame in the upper arm, and unfit for further military service. This is attested by me, as requested, in line of duty.

    In the barracks   J. J. Heidelbach
    At Winter Hill
    24 March 1778

Letters to the Prince

Sir, Gracious Colonel and Court Marshal

As due to unfavorable circumstances I have been put in such a condition that I can not longer serve in the campaign, even if the present cure is successful, which according to the opinion of our Regimental Surgeon Heidelbach seems unlikely. Therefore, I take my only recourse sir, in order to be worthy of your future favor, and lay the most humble enclosure at His Highness' feet, so that I can confidently await a quick, gratifying, and most gracious resolution. I am convinced of your high-minded disposition, therefore, I dare to inconvenience you, sir, with this humble written request to His Highness in the confident assurance that he would never be able to leave his throne without giving a hearing to the most humble request of an officer, an officer who was unfortunate in the service against the enemy.

In this flattering hope, I strive with the most sincere attention to be

In the barracks near Boston at Winter Hill 23 March 1778

Sir,
Your most humble servant,
Carl Dittmar Spangenberg

Letters to the Prince

Most Illustrious Landgrave
and Hereditary Prince,
Gracious Sovereign and Lord!

During the affair at Bennington on 16 August 1777, I was unfortunately wounded in the right shoulder, and I must thank the good care and untiring efforts of our Regimental Surgeon Heidelbach for my life, even though I am lame in my right arm, which makes me unfit for further service.

Your Highness will already be graciously familiar with my most humble representation from the reports submitted, and my most humble written request, as well as the accompanying attestation, but the present situation, complicated by the distance from Europe, makes it easy for problems to arise, so that the reports and my most humble request could have been lost, so I take the most humble liberty to repeat my request and seek my recall once again and most humbly.

It is, most gracious Prince, not cowardice nor a lack of willingness to perform duty that forces me to this, but true need and misfortune. For the Prince, who has always shown such favor for me, I would be more than willing to lay down my life if things were otherwise. I recommend myself to this continued favor, and remain with the most sincerely respectful attention,

    Winter Hill   Your Serene Highness'
    10 October 1778   Most humble servant,
                         Carl Dittmar Spangenberg

- - - - - - -

    Most Illustrious Hereditary Prince,
      Gracious Sovereign and Lord!

Your Highness, I would have risked this most submissive written report earlier if I had not always had the hope, from one month to the next, that the sad situation of the company graciously entrusted to me would soon change, and I would have the pleasure of laying myself at Your Highness' feet with a somewhat more cheerful heart. My entire soul, from the past winter to the spring of this year, has been disturbed by the frightful losses, which among the entire corps were especially suffered by my company. All active care which I, as well as the company chief, as a loyal subject of Your Highness, have employed to check the increase, was fruitless, and unfortunate fate, moreover, at that time, was that my and Captain von Schelm's Companies had their winter quarters on a height close to the North River, where a continuous storm wind beat against us, which caused the most healthy men, let alone the troops who were extremely fatigued from the recent sea voyage, and various similarly endured fatigues on land, to suffer. To add to their misery, they were poorly dressed.

To reduce this last inconvenience, I exhausted every bit of my energy, and obtained the necessary clothing for my men, myself, in every possible way. My own situation during this miserable time was even sadder, because I alone had to care for the company, because both junior officers had died, and my 1st Lieutenant [Carl Philipp] Eytelwein, during these most dangerous conditions, lay sick for three-fourths of a year. Praise God that we survived so long, and that the terrible sickness let up, and that during the present year, I have prospects of hopefully better winter quarters in which to see the rest of my company in more permanent conditions, as the most humble duty requirement, with which I will never cease to sacrifice myself for Your Highness, should be contributed with complete loyalty.

May it most graciously please Your Highness that I recommend myself to Your Highness' further benevolence with this opportunity, and that I express the most humble wish that it might please Your Highness to extend the ever-special favor of serving in Your Highness' house, away from this land full of sad designs, again near your lofty person, and be most graciously put in such a position that I can again be the provider for a wife and three minor children.

I strive in most sincere devotion to be

In camp	Your Serene Highness'
At Morris' House	Most humble servant,
York Island	C. D. Spangenberg
8 November 1782	Captain

- - - - - - -

Most Illustrious Hereditary Prince,
Gracious Sovereign of the Land and Lord!

Your Highness, I had the pleasure during the month of November of last year, to indicate my humbleness. Presently the death of Major Scheel gives me the opportunity to lay myself at Your Highness' feet, and to recommend myself most humbly to the most gracious master of my country.

Your Highness was so kind during our march out of Hanau, as to give me hope that I would not always remain in America, but would be recalled at an opportune time, and there I should be provided for by the land, as consolation.

Might Your Highness still cherish this gracious intention for an old, loyal servant of Your Highness' house, and grant me a gracious plea for more opportunity for continued service to Your Highness' person, than offered in this sad land, and to prove my limitless devotion, with which I strive to be

  In Quarters Your Serene Highness'
  Oyster Bay Most humble servant,
  Long Island C. D. Spangenberg
  4 March 1783

- - - - - - -

Sir, Gracious Court Marshal

As I am the only officer in this part of the world who has been released from captivity - now on parole - and I know that in the present situation you could have received no news about the Convention troops, I take the liberty most humbly to notify you of my exchange.

On 24 September, all the captive officers received orders to assemble in Rutland. Some of them were commanded by General von Riedesel to remain by the captive German regiments of the Northern Army. The rest however, were to go to their designated places. On 2 October, we arrived at Providence, near the rebel General [John] Sullivan. After he gave the order to the commissary, we went to Warwick, where we rented a ship for 100 paper Reichsthalers of our own money, and were taken to Newport on it. We arrived there on 4 October. Immediately upon my arrival I heard that Cannoneer [Valentin] Raab, who had performed duty with the rebels, himself had been captured during the last expedition. I reported this to the general at once, and he ordered me to take Raab to New York. At my departure, Raab was deathly sick and I had to leave him behind in the hospital. On 7 October, an officer and a private of the Brunswick troops, Bombardier Hestermann and Non-commissioned Officer Knittel of Your Highness, our most gracious Prince's, troops arrived at Newport, from Canada with the equipment and uniform items. A flag of truce was prepared at once to go to Boston. [Charles Hector], Count d'Estaing however, would not grant permission for it to enter the harbor at Boston. Therefore, as the entire Convention [Army] was now on the march to Virginia, it was said the equipment should sail there. Late on the eighteenth, we received orders to sail to New York with a rather large fleet of

Letters to the Prince

54 transport ships, a frigate, and a privateer. We arrived at Hellgate on the seventeenth [sic], and went to New York in small boats. Here I found Cannoneer Faulstroh and Musketeer Iffland of the Major's Company, who had taken service with the enemy, and then deserted from them. Supposedly a large shipment of Germans and Englanders, including Non-commissioned Officer Buss, another non-commissioned officer and private, and Cannoneers Nordt and Stenger, were transferred, and had gone with Lieutenant Colonel Speth to Canada. Every day, numerous men of the Convention [Army], which is marching to Virginia, report in, more than 150 in five days.

Lieutenant General Clinton, a few days ago, undertook an expedition up the North River, which these poor individuals must cross in order to recapture a brigade, or division. Washington discovered the intent too early, however, detached a part of his army, and had it march behind the advance. Therefore, General Clinton returned from the expedition yesterday. The Cannoneers [Michael] Paul and Lockmann, Jr., died in captivity. Reportedly there are many, non-commissioned officers, as well as musketeers and cannoneers, serving with the rebels, but who intend at the first opportunity to do what the others have done. I also have a map of the region of Rhode Island to send to You. I can not show the maneuvers of the enemy, as I was still in captivity at that time. The second line, which in actual siege operations - and which together with the fort, was called Fort Pfennig by the rebels, was made after the siege and is the main defense at present, has been developed very advantageously. This I have indicated. My instruments and books and what little equipment I had, was taken from me by the rebels during the unfortunate affair at Williams Cook, near Bennington, and that is the reason why I can not provide you with a detailed map. As soon as I am in a position to obtain a case of instruments, I will be able to draw more maps with which, most humbly to serve you. With the most humble request, that you sir, might have thoughts of me at the start of the event, as in this case I can turn to no one better than you, and have proof of your satisfaction for my father's entire house. Therefore, I ask you once again to allow me to lay myself at His Highness' feet.

    I have the honor, with true attention, to remain

Letters to the Prince

New York
7 December 1778

Sir,
Your completely dedicated Servant,
[Johann Michael] Bach

Letters to the Prince

Most Illustrious Landgrave,
Gracious Hereditary Prince and Lord!

Your Highness, need finally forces me most humbly to lay this most humble presentation at Your Highness' most gracious feet, because since 16 August 1777 chain of large and small problems, following quickly one after the other, which each time was accompanied with bitter loss and damage, have torn me apart without me having the least blame. If Your Highness has the most benevolence and patience, I would dare present a detailed account with all the incidental circumstances, of which none were pleasant, but only unfortunate, which I have had to tolerate from time to time, and which up to the spring of this year, were continuous. I call upon the witness of my major and all my other comrades, all of whom know the circumstances and can best confirm the truth, of the account, which necessity forces me herewith to lay at Your Highness' feet in most sincere devotion.

On 16 August 1777, I was captured on the field of the battle, during the unfortunate affair at Bennington, badly mistreated and completely plundered. I tried to borrow money from Brunswick officers - because, as I was the only Hesse-Hanau officer, I had to seek relief and help from strangers. With [the money] I again bought the most essential items and thereafter I was embarrassed, and had to do my own laundry in the river. No sooner did I have this least little bit, than the rebels again stole everything, and once again I was in the same position that I had been after the plundering on the field of battle. Following that, we were all brought together on a prison ship, treated very badly thereon, and especially, as I am a Hessian against whom the rebels are very bitter, I would have been lost without the protection of the other Brunswick officers. From the prison ship, we were taken to Westminster, in Massachusetts Bay, receiving quarters initially, but fed with Negro food, and still badly treated. Eventually, we received some money through a flag of truce from Winter Hill, from our respective regiments and corps. Thereafter, no one could receive lodging or entertainment without paying. We had to pay dearly for everything, even to the point of extravagance, and the most necessary small clothes and uniform items were at such a price that they could hardly be afforded. In October 1778, we went with a flag of truce to New York, at our own expense, in the hope of being exchanged, but after many hopeful promises of a speedy exchange by His Excellency, Sir Henry Clinton, we had to undertake our return voyage to our enemies, who then believed that we had brought much money with us, and in consideration, the quarters and other necessities became much more barbaric than before. Then we were led through various provinces, and all of Pennsylvania, again at our own expense, as it pleased the farmers and administrators there to charge so much for the quarters and necessities, as well as for the wagons, as to be cruel. This did not change until the fortunate time of our exchange, when all the inhabitants, with and without character, gave us the final blow, and sought to profit therefrom in a revengeful manner, so that when I embarked at Elizabethtown, to cross to New York, they also took all my silver, but for the return of my very few belongings, I gave a hardy thanks to Most Holy Providence. Now here I was once again, in order to present myself without blushing, at their distain of strangers for my uniform items, which were not only of the most gracious diverse colors, but still more by their wretchedness, and for an appearance unlike that of an officer, unwillingly asking, with an oppressed heart, for another advanced payment, only sufficient so that visibly I would be able to perform duty in the most gracious character of a 2nd lieutenant, because my captain had not yet been exchanged, but was in Virginia.

May it please Your Highness, most graciously to see, and most graciously to forgive all this, my fate, being laid at Your Highness' most gracious feet. How great the difference is for the losses between the war prisoners and the Convention prisoners, but not in the manner in which all of us find ourselves as captives, in which the loss by one is the same as that of the other among the rebels, and all that pertains to those disreputable and negligent in their duty names. The difference for the Convention was that a portion of their quarters money, and also until the end of 1780, of their forage money, was retained in New York. However, we were plundered and sometimes robbed and mistreated by our uncivilized escort, which each, who was in a great mass together, could not prevent. I therefore, lost, despite my constant attention, and even here in Canada, where I was assisted by Lieutenant Colonel von Creuzbourg and my major, first - the quarters money for my entire time here, second - the transport of equipment, and third - I lose the total amount of forage money paid out to the Convention [prisoners], as well as the loss of all my baggage in the action, which at the same time, I was wounded above the eye by a grazing shot, and placed in the embarrassment of losing an eye, if the regimental surgeon of the Brunswick Dragoons had not given me exceptional care, causing his own misfortune of being captured with me, but fortunate for me. After making myself, in appearance, fit for duty with the most necessary items, but without my sash, and resuming activity, as we were to vacate our winter quarters at Kamourasca, and enter camp at Point Levi, another unexpected misfortune occurred, when several bateaux sank during a storm, including one in which my entire baggage and belongings were, and all new, very expensive, and only recently replaced. They included large and small uniform items which were ruined and made unfit for wear. To this, was added that there was no hope of receiving anything from our governor, who listened to all my complaints and assured me of a resolution [of my problem] within two months, but of which nothing has come, but still less can I expect any favorable results for me. May it please Your Highness at the same time, during this coming year, graciously to order that Your Highness' artillery officers of Your Highness' Infantry Regiment 1st Battalion, in consideration of their monthly pay on the same scale, which was originally the case, but later was increased during the thirteenth month, and also by the extra allowance of a batman. Neither Colonel von Gall nor my then captain knew about the Artillery however, and without definite orders, would not pay it to me, nor to my comrades. On the other hand, they assured us that they would most humbly report this and ask the reason. Therefore, because of this, it is an important consideration to me, so that my wound can heal, to lay most humbly at Your Highness' feet, and once again in most sincere devotion, to request that I and the other officers of a similar character of the 1st Battalion, from that time to the present and henceforth, be made equal, and may it please Your Highness, taking my other and most unfortunate fates into most gracious and most enlightened consideration, to clear them away, so that all the noted needs are eliminated, and save me so I can conduct myself and be like a proper officer, the same as the others.

In the most humble hope of a gracious acceptance, I lay myself at Your Highness' most gracious feet, and in the most sincere submission, remain

In camp at   Your Serene Highness
Point Levi   My most gracious Prince of the land
3 October 1782   and Lord's
    Most humble servant,
    The-up-to-the-present, 2nd Lieutenant
    Johann Michael Bach

That all this concerning the misfortunes which befell the good Lieutenant Bach is as stated, and his request that I submit this most humble memorial, which he lays at Your Highness' gracious feet, I most humbly attest in line of duty and with certainty.

    Your Serene Highness'
    Most humble servant,
    G. Pausch

[I have not translated pages 375-377, containing a letter written at Halifax on 18 January 1783, by le Blanc, which is in French. BEB]

Letters to the Prince

Most Illustrious Sovereign,
Gracious Hereditary Prince and Lord!

On 10 March, after several days of illness, Major Scheel died. Therefore, Lieutenant Colonel von Janecke ordered that pending further most gracious orders, I was to assume the duties of the dead man.

May it please Your Highness, as long as I have the honor to be in Your Highness' service, to allow me always to recommend myself most humbly to Your Highness' memory, as throughout my life, I remain in most sincere humiliation

Oyster Bay	Your Serene Highness'
Long Island	Most humble servant,
14 March 1783	F. v. Francke
	Captain

- - - - - - -

Letters to the Prince

Most Serene Highness,
Gracious Sovereign and Lord!

Your Highness, I most humbly report how we sailed from Bremerlehe on 10 May, and without entering an English harbor, arrived here in New York on 11 August. We constantly had favorable winds and would have completed our voyage in nine weeks if our commodore had not chased prizes [French and American] ships. We passed New York and sailed so far to the south that we left Charleston behind us. The heat was unbearable, all the water foul, scurvy and putrid fever were rampant. The ship *Ester*, on which I was with my, men had eighteen dead. The misfortune was much greater than I present. I brought the men most graciously entrusted to me on the ship, fresh, healthy, and clean. But I think back on the embarkation of the Free Corps with horror. The ship on which I was, held 200 men, 150 of which were men of the Free Corps. I required of all the companies, that each company cleanse itself, and here, the real dregs of the entire corps came together, men who had already become half-dead from vermin and rash. This was not enough. The ship was converted to a hospital and 22 dangerously ill individuals were brought on board. The ship was the largest in the entire fleet and had no ventilation, so that soon there was a full contagiousness. I had already complained about my needs to Captain Hense in Bremerlehe, and I thought I would not be able to save a man therefrom. Aboard ship I did not lose a man, but on land, since 28 September, when the first one died, I have lost six men, namely:

1. Christian Gottfried, from Eckartsberge in Saxony, [5 feet], 5 and 1/2 inches tall.

2. Konrad Schreiber, from Cronau in Hesse, 7 and 3/4 inches

3. Johannes Voeller, from Angersbach in Riedesel, 6 and 1/4 inches

4. Johannes Schranckel, from Offenbach, 5 inches

5. Heinrich Boemmer, from Cuxhaven in Hesse, 3 and 1/2 inches

6. Johann Georg Bick, from Nassau in Weilburg, 1 inch.

The fleet to Canada had already sailed, and all the recruits must remain here during the winter. I lay myself once again, most humbly, at Your Highness' feet in appreciation of so many great favors, and I wish nothing more than the opportunity make myself worthy of Your Highness' continued benevolence.

New York Your Serene Highness'
16 October 1781 Most humble servant,
 Lieutenant Buenau

- - - - - - -

Most Illustrious Prince, Gracious Lord!
Your Highness, allow me to submit the most humble report about the command so graciously

Letters to the Prince

entrusted to me. The entire force, consisting of 2 non-commissioned officers and 42 privates are all well, and nothing has occurred since the last most humble report, except that I moved into camp with my command, near Brooklyn, two miles from New York, on 11 August. The French fleet, from the West Indies, has been seen in the waters outside New York, since 30 July. I remain with the most humble devotion

    In camp   Your Serene Highness'
    Near Brooklyn   Most humble servant,
    3 August 1782   Lieutenant Buenau,
                  of the Jaeger Corps

- - - - - - -

Most Illustrious Prince, Gracious Lord!

Your Highness, I report, most humbly, that on today's date, I went on board the ship with the name *John*, with my command, and since my last most humbler report, nothing has changed.

I lay myself with the most sincere devotion, as long as I live, at Your Highness' feet.

    New York   Lieutenant Buenau
    24 August 1782

- - - - - - -

Letters to the Prince

Most Illustrious Landgrave,
And Hereditary Prince,
Gracious Sovereign and Lord!

At the time when I dedicated myself to Your Highness' service, and had the pleasure of being assigned to Your Highness' regiment as regimental quartermaster, I believed my finances to be adequate to what my duty required. I was only assuming that the pay graciously given to me, without adding my own [money] thereto, would be adequate to keep me solvent. I had hardly started for America when I saw I had been deceived in my preconceived ideas. Therefore I did everything to show my Prince my eagerness and loyalty for the service, neither fatigue nor work could discourage me. Colonel von Gall gave me orders to compile pay lists from 1 May 1776 to 24 June 1777, through a variety of details, first according to the Hanau play scale, and secondly, according to the English pay scale, though this took me an uninterrupted six weeks, in the end it caused only purposeless work. Still this did not cause me to lose patience. I would have done everything that duty and the most humble respect demanded, in order to make myself worthy of my Prince's favor. However, I saw the dispersal of my private wealth, due to the many travel costs and expenses related to my service, and finally, also a disorder in my calculations throughout, and this is the reason that I most humbly sought my discharge in September 1777.

As my pay, before we entered captivity, was insufficient for my subsistence, it may please Your Highness readily to understand that later in a county, where everything is exceptionally expensive, when the bonus money was withheld from us, when the pay did not follow in gold, when we had to accept paper money for bills at the greatest loss, instead of pay, therefore it was simply not possible to make ends meet. Now the work has been increased, also. By a gracious directive of 23 September 1776, the Brunswick pay scale was adopted. This project was barely completed, I hardly believed that I had my calculations in order, when due to another directive of 10 November, the regiment was given a guide. In accordance with the aforesaid directive, officers and middle staff personnel remained on the Hanau play scale. On the other hand, the non-commissioned officers and privates on the Brunswick pay scale, and as a result, a task with unending variations, and work was again opened. As all these directives concern that portion of the regiment now in Canada, but remained unknown to them for many long years, in the end, when everything had to balance, I could already see that my ability, if I did not want anything else to become confused, would be insufficient, and that during a prolonged campaign, or stay in America, the previous pay would be reduced by the last directive of November 1777, and the little more which I had under the Brunswick pay scale, would be taken away. At the same time, also, I was transferred from Captain Scheel's Company, where I was actually assigned, and I clearly looked ruin in the face. Therefore, Your Highness, grant that I may again lay myself at Your Highness' feet and again request my discharge. I will acknowledge this great favor with the most humble thanks, and with the most sincere respect, strive to be

    Virginia   Your Serene Highness'
    Albemarle County   Most humble servant,
    Barracks   Sartorius
    23 November 1780

- - - - - - -

Most Illustrious Hereditary Prince,
Gracious Sovereign and Lord!

May it please Your Highness to allow me to present that I, Johannes Moerschell, entered Your Highness' service already in 1762, and during that time have sought to demonstrate loyalty and obedience toward my superiors and my service to the best of my ability.

Now, in the time when we were not yet in captivity, I served with the greatest pleasure, so even after a long time in captivity, until we were transferred to Virginia, when I was not in a condition to do what was ordered of me, and which did not seem important.

Letters to the Prince

Therefore on 8 April 1789, I was unexpectedly shouted at by a cannoneer from about 200 yards from my barracks, that I was to report to Captain Pausch. When I arrived, two non-commissioned officers were ordered to hold me, and on his orders, had to hold me, and the captain himself performed the punishment, without asking or telling me my crime, or what I had done, other than to chastise me, and strike me with the flat of his sword. I was so confounded that I, having received about twenty blows, sank to the ground and surrendered to the heavy hands. However, that was not enough, but according to what the men told the captain, I wanted to join the scoundrels, that I was no longer of any value in this life, and was of little consequence. So I received sixty or seventy blows without an investigation or my knowing what wrong I had committed, nor could I learn before the punishment, why I had to put up with such a cruel punishment.

I therefore, found it necessary, according to my poor condition in eight days, before I could walk again, as I had no other choice remaining, and if I wanted to preserve my life, than to commit perjury. This was unpleasant for an individual who had served eighteen years. [This seems to indicate that he broke his oath by deserting.]

However, thereafter, since that time, I have had few healthy days and seldom find myself in a

Letters to the Prince

condition to perform Your Highness' service. Therefore, I most humbly ask Your Highness for my discharge, because I have met a friend here in Quebec who has offered to keep me until my death, because I find myself unfit for service. There were reasons enough to maintain my perjury, which however, never crossed my mind, and I would rather have suffered death, if I had not thought to redeem myself, and to go to Canada, where we arrived on 16 June 1780 at Quebec, in Canada, and because I reported with the troops to Captain von Schoell, he assigned me the command over the artillery which was present there.

I remain with the most sincere resolve

In camp at Your Serene Highness'
St. Michael Most humble servant,
1 October 1780 Johannas Moerschell
 Bombardier

[The End]

INDEX

----, Charles Hector 173 Christian Ludwig 26 Lord Charles 33
ACKERMANN, Karen 13
ALTER, Friedrich 34
AMAND, Adam 54
AMHERST, Lord 35
ANDRES, Joahnnes 116
ANGERSBACH, 19
AUFFLEIDER, Musketeer 133
BACH, Johann Michael 176 182 Lt 182
BACUMERTH, 155
BAECKER, Musketter 131
BAILEY, Capt 159
BAUER, Musketeer 49 51-52
BECKER, Corp 65 68 71 Georg 61
BEIER, Musketeer 56
BELLINGER, Corp 118 Johannes 117
BICK, Johann Georg 185
BICKES, 160 Conrad 159 Musketeer 161
BINMUELLER, Grenadier 150
BISCHHAUSEN, 155
BODE, Peter 39
BOECKEL, Friedrich 11
BOEMMER, Heinrich 185
BOHLAENDER, Johann Adam 134 Pvt 135 137
BRAUMANN, Johann 34
BREIDENBACH, Wilhelm 114
BRUCHAUSEN, 118
BRUCKMANN, Philipp 20
BRUNSWICK, Duke Of 86 100 136 152-153
BRUST, Musketter 68 Vice-corp 71
BUENAU, Lt 185-186
BURCKHARD, Cadet 124 126 136 Ensign 124 133 155 Ludwig Theodor 24 158 160
BURGOYNE, 40 115 135 Gen 36 John 17
BUSCH, Free Corp 50 61
BUSS, Corp 65 68 71 Free Corp 65 Noncomissioned Officer 174

BUTLER, 115
CARLETON, Gen 48 Guy 40 86 91-92 96 100 104 Lt Gen 88
CLARKE, Alfred 100 Brig Gen 104 107
CLINTON, Gen 174 Henry 31 178 Lt Gen 174
CONRADI, Jerome 26 Lt 27-28
CORNWALLIS, Earl 33
CREUZBOURG, Lt Col 39 52
D'ESTAING, Count 173
DAEFNER, 118
DAVID, Henrich 118
DEHNHARD, Christoph 158
DEPHNER, Grenadier 49
DESHMER, Georg 118
DIEHL, 160-161 Christoph 159
DIEMAR, 33
DIGBY, Robert 91
DUFAIS, 155 Wilhelm 145 147-148
ECKHARDT, 138
EICHEL, Johann 39
EIDEBENZ, Henrich 1
ELZER, Joseph 51
EMMERICH, Andreas 32 Col 34
EMMERT, 116 Andreas 5
ESCHWEGE, Lt 5 24
EWALD, 160 Corp 12 16 Musketeer 54 Peter 11
EYTELWEIN, Carl Philipp 170
FARQUES, Lt 31
FAULSTROH, Cannoneer 174 Heinrich 34
FISCHER, Henrich 1 112 Musketeer 112
FISHER, Musketeer 113
FIX, Musketeer 65 Peter 65
FLACHSHAAR, Ludwig 96
FLUECKMANN, Jacob 118
FOERSTER, Musketeer 71
FRANCKE, F V 183
FREUND, Grenadier Jr 54
FREYENSOEHNER, Georg 67
FRITZ, Grenadier 150

FUHR, Georg Conrad 19 Musketeer 129
GATES, Horatio 16
GEISMAR, 35
GERLACH, Capt 163
GERMAIN, George 35
GEWALD, Jacob 135
GIESE, Drummer 119 135 137 Wilhelm 83
GOTS, Drummer 34
GOTTFRIED, Christian 185
GOTTSCHALK, Surgeon 96 116 Wilhelm 11 89
GOTZ, Drummer 32
GRIMM, Musketeer 125 127 Wilhelm 22 77
GRUENEWALD, Grenadier 44
HAEMERLE, Musketeer 49
HALDIMAND, Frederick 42 Gen 44-47 51 57-58 60 71-73
HALLARSCHKA, Johannes 78
HALLATSCHKA, Musketeer 126 128-129 133 136 158 Pvt 135
HALLE, Musketeer 34 Pvt 32
HALLERSCHKA, Musketeer 131
HANDEL, Johann 64
HASSLER, Friedrich 118
HAUMANN, Free Corp 66 Jacob 34
HAYMANN, Jacob 12
HEERWAGEN, 153 155 Jacob 124
HEIDELBACH, J J 166 Jeremiah 3 Surgeon 70 164-165 167-168
HEINTZINGER, Musketeer 136 158 Philipp 135
HEISTERREICH, Sgt 76
HENSE, Capt 42 47 184
HENSEL, Sgt 61
HENZEL, Henrich 53 Quartermaster Sgt 56 68
HERBER, Michael 17
HERMANN, Johann 10 Musketeer 19
HERRMANN, Musketeer 121
HESITERREICH, Sgt 52
HESSLER, Christoph 118
HESTERMANN, Bombardier 34 40 54 66 68 173 Carl Friedrich 9
HEYL, 160 Philipp Jacob 159 161
HINCKEL, Philipp 125

HOENE, Mudwig 16
HOLLAND, Maj 60 73-74
HUEFFNER, Musketeer 133
HUFFNER, 66
IFFLAND, Johann 34 Musketeer 174
INSDORF, Christoph 116 George Jr 78 George Sr 78 Hautboist Jr 133 Hautboist Sr 80 83 133
JAHN, Johann 64
JANECKE, 27 Lt Col 137
JUNG, Friedrich 159 Lt 160
KAISER, Friedrich 135
KASIER, Pvt 137
KEMPEL, Lt Col 85
KEMPF, Caspar 78 Musketeer 133
KEMPFFER, Ensign 46 51 Friedrich Ludwig 43 Friedrich Ludwug 154
KING, Theodor 118
KIRCHKOFF, Capt-at-arms 159
KIRCHOFF, Adam 75 Capt-at-arms 162
KITZ, Drummer 128 133 Georg 127
KITZLEBEN, Carl August 159
KLEE, Leonard 116
KNITTEL, Noncomissioned Officer 173 Sgt 31 34 40 54 68
KOCH, Andreas 163
KOEHLER, 18 Heinrich 81 Musketeer 102
KOHLEP, 161 Adam 61 Caspar 78 Corp 65 Georg 1 Musketeer 133 Pvt 89
KOHLEY, 160
KOLEP, Musketeer 159
KRAFT, Andreas 18
KREBS, Conrad 21
KRIEG, Conrad 8 78 Lance Corp 135 Musketeer 133 136 Pvt 137
KUEHN, Musketeer 73 121
LANGHARD, 34
LEBLANC, 182
LEICK, Musketeer 65
LENTZ, 28 Carl 78 Col 75 81-82 84 114 121 133-134 136 138 163 Johannn Christoph 24 Lt 158 Lt Col 133 157 Quartermaster Sgt 11
LENZ, Henrich 1 Quartermaster Sgt 115
LEONHARD, Musketeer 51-52
LOCKMANN, Cannoneer Jr 174

LOSSBERG, Young 107
MAHR, Georg Sr 112 Musketeer 112-113 Philipp 78
MAUL, 102
MENCK, Musketeer 65 Philipp 65
MERZ, Cannoneer 53 56
MEYER, Friedrich 114
MIECKEL, Musketeer 54
MOERSCHEL, Bombardier 66
MOERSCHELL, Johann 33 Johannas 191 Johannes 189
MUELLER, 162 Adam 78 102 117 Hautboist 133 Jacob 160 Joachim 75 Musketeer 49
NENTZEL, Eckhard 103
NEUBERGER, August 86
NIEMAYER, Maj 151
NORDT, Cannoneer 174
NORTH, Lord 105-106 108
ORBIG, Corp 50
ORTH, Conrad 102 Corp 65 68 71 Heinrich 9 Johannes 61 Sgt 11
OTTO, Samuel 68
PAUL, Michael 174
PAUSCH, Capt 74 190 G 182 Georg 25
PHILLIPS, Gen 36 Maj Gen 35 143 William 31
POHL, Nicolaus 104
PORT, Musketeer 51-52
PULFER, Musketeer 51-52
RAAB, Johannes 116 Valentin 173
REIF, Cannoneer 64 68 73
REINECKE, Lt 86
REMMY, Michael 9 Musketeer 20 115 Pvt 119
RIEDESEL, Gen 40
ROPP, Johann 34
RUEFFER, 104 Daniel 102
RUEHL, 160-161 Philipp 159
SARTORIOUS, Carl August 54
SARTORIUS, 155 189 Lt 156 Quartermaster 156
SCHAEFFER, Philipp 11 26 41 Sgt 53-54 56 58 60 64
SCHAUBERGER, Johann 8
SCHAUER, Theophile 121
SCHEEL, 155 Capt 25-26 44 54 75 189 Carl August 24 Maj 25-28 171 183

SCHENOT, 66
SCHLEGEL, Grenadier 150
SCHLINGELLOF, Grenadier 106-107
SCHMIDT, Jacob 13 15 118 Nich 118
SCHNEIDER, Grenadier II 150 Herinrich 34
SCHOELL, Capt 114 124-125
SCHRANCKEL, Johannes 185
SCHREIBER, Konrad 185
SCHROEDER, Drummer 49
SCHUBERT, Musketeer 8
SCHUETTEN, Wilhelm 61
SCHUNCK, Capt 151
SCHWAB, Adam 44
SCHWEINEBRATEN, Adj 138 Nicolaus 138
SCHWEINSBERGER, Hieronymous 9 Musketeer 129
SEEBACH, Conrad 120
SEIFFERT, Lt 38 40 43 46 58 64
SELTZER, Johannes 133
SENTZELL, Johann 34
SICKENBERGER, Johann 16
SIEBERT, Henrich 34
SPAHN, Corp 51
SPANGENBERG, C D 171-172 Carl Dittmar 165-166 169
SPANIER, Musketeer 121
SPENGLER, 10 18 Georg 9
SPETH, Lt Col 174
STEIN, Musketeer 102 Peter 78
STELLER, Lt 151
STENGER, Cannoneer 174
STORCK, Musketter 68 Vice-corp 71
SULLIVAN, John 173
TACK, Corp 117-118 Jacob 71
TEMPELL, Georg 16 115 Musketeer 115
THOMA, Lt 74 158-159
TRAUT, Conrad 102 Phillipp 114
TROTT, Lt 124
UNGAR, Andreas Sr 54 Georg Carl 16 68 Vice-corp 71
VAUPEL, Corp 5 Quartermaster Sgt 9 11 53-54 65 Samuel 8 Sgt 61 119 Sgt Maj 19-20 98 115
VELDEN, August 67
VETTER, Lorentz 94
VOELLER, Johannes 185

VONBAURMEISTER, Carl Leopold 107
VONBORCK, Henrich Christian 66
VONBUTTLAR, 30 123-124 127-128 130 132 134 136-137 139 155 Capt 25 77 Lt 5 7 9 20 Maurice 1
VONCREUZBOURG, Col 86 Lt Col 45 50 52 56 60 62 64-66 68 73-74 180
VONDIEMAR, Ernst Friedrich 32
VONESCHWEGE, 79 155 Capt 119 Christian 1 83 85 87 91 93 95 97 100 103 105 107 109 112-113 First Lt 124 137 Lt 132 Second Lt 124 Staff Capt 80-81 114
VONFRANCKE, Jost Friedrich 109
VONGALL, Col 20 25 32 40-41 54 67 123 125 127 129-130 141 152 156 181 187 Commander 156 Ensign 105 115 W R 36 Wilhelm Rudolph 4
VONGEISMAR, 34 Capt 36 Friedrich 33
VONGERMANN, 155 Capt 26 28 124-125 Friedrich 2-4 6 8 10 13-15 18-19 21-24 26 30
VONGEYLING, 155
VONHACHENBURG, Carl Wilhelm 92
VONHOHORST, Ludwig 43
VONJANECKE, Lt Col 137 183 Michael 24
VONKNYPHAUSEN, 66 72 Lt Gen 136 Wilhelm 33
VONLEININGEN, Count 26-27
VONLINDAU, 116 119-120 Carl 114 117 122
VONLOOS, Johann 66
VONLOSSBERG, 66 Friedrich Wilhelm 88 Lt Gen 89-90 92 102 104 106-107
VONMEYER, Lt 9
VONNOTTEN, 160
VONPAPE, Franz 9 Free Corp 12 17 Wilhelm 150
VONPASSERN, Ludwig 38 Ludwig Wilhelm 37
VONRAUSCHENPLAT, Col 62
VONREICHE, 111
VONRICHTERSLEBEN, 155
VONRIEDESEL, Friedrich Adolf 5 Gen 163 172 Maj Gen 31-32 36

VONSCHACHTEN, Friedrich 23
VONSCHACHTER, 141 Friedrich 140 142
VONSCHELM, 27 Capt 169 Christian Ludwig 26
VONSCHLAGENTEUFEL, Capt 66
VONSCHOELL, Capt 123 160 162 191 F L 42 45 48 57 59 62 68 72 74-75 77 Friedrich Ludwig 30
VONSEITZ, 50
VONSPETH, Ernst 62
VONSUCCOW, Lt 150
VONTROTT, 155 Lt 20
VONWESTERHAGEN, 27 Thylo 26
VONWEYHERS, 155 Ensign 124 Ernst 1 Second Lt 124 137
WALD, Musketeer 102
WASHINGTON, 174 George 88
WEBER, Caspar 50 Musketeer 67 Peter 12 89
WEINGARTEN, 127 Friedrich 117 Musketeer 125 131
WEISS, Sgt 74 Surgeon 44 70
WEITZEL, 155 Grenadier 51 Johann 67 Johannes 77
WELOW, 40
WERLING, Musketeer 52
WETTER, 159-160 Musketeer 162
WEYHERS, Second Lt 135
WIEDERHOLD, Capt 151
WILHELM, Johann 53
WILLOE, 40
WISKEMANN, 102 Christopher 19 Musketeer 129 133
WOLF, Musketeer 53
WOOD, Col 78 James 78
ZEH, Caspar 118
ZEHNER, Adolph 10
ZINCKE, Lt 151
ZIPF, Carl Friedrich 9

www.ingramcontent.com/pod-product-compliance
Lightning Source LLC
Chambersburg PA
CBHW071417160426
43195CB00013B/1719